Hebelteleskop

Proem

0a

one day i wrote HEBELTELESKOP upon the strand
but came the waves and washèd it away,
alas,
a nothing
in this cosmos
hebelteleskop
a long poem about vanity
vanity of the long poem
vanity of the poet hebelteleskop
a canadian, one of the nothings, a cosmos
in progress a long poem hebelteleskop
to be assembled using the twitter archive
of @hebelteleskop in 2017,
this is the dream hebelteleskop speaking

in hebelteleskop to be assembled
using the twitter archive of @hebelteleskop in 2017.
a canadian, one of the nothings, a cosmos.
we got better as the game went on (see hebelteleskop 3k)
but we needed to take advantage of our chances
we have to score more goals.
making hebelteleskop and sharing as it is made, the video
hebelteleskop tonight is stabbed multiple times
hebel
vancouver canucks score
teleskop ...
discovering 15 asteroids, a periodic comet
as well as hundreds of variable stars
star clusters
galaxy clusters
and a galaxy supercluster.
and pluto in his life
hebelteleskop.
vancouver,
british columbia,
canada,
the earth,
goodnight:
portrait of hebelteleskop
as a young teleskop
dwelling in goodnight
hebelteleskop is a world
among many dreamt in goodnight
pelicans just burned 15 seconds
while losing and the shot clock off unreal

hebelteleskop is a world
among many dreamt in goodnight so hebelteleskop
familiar and mysterious
as the full 'boring moon'
the complete mapping of all
is vanity
asteroids
their cameras have become windows
survey of its features
meteorite impacts
surface of mercury (see hebelteleskop 3s),
venus, its atmosphere,
survive
to be hebelteleskop
on a cosmic
this is the dream hebelteleskop speaking
one day i wrote HEBELTELESKOP upon the strand
but came the waves and washèd it away
vanity of the long poem
vanity of the poet
hebelteleskop

0c

delusional
his long poem the worst long poem,
hebelteleskop brewing co.
to infuse fizz in his
thank cannabis for hebelteleskop.
so it begins in february 2016 of goodnight
and made in 2017
and we're off.
handmade in 2017
a year in the life of humanity, hebelteleskop
in the year of the monkey
vernon drive grocery
vancouver taxi
unemployed hebelteleskop
underused, underrated
in the game
of hebel
induce hebelteleskop
trash this long poem by hebelteleskop
the long poem
of vancouver b.c.
eternally he
hebelteleskop i thought an unclassifiable fish
roll the dice
that number is the number of lines in your stanza
the second number is the number of feet in the first line
hebelteleskop
just setting up my twitter
soon hebelteleskop an instrument used to aid the soul or camera in knowing or photographing distant objects

the hebelteleskop view of earth distant vancouver of goodnight
as a heavenly hebelteleskop my paradiso a space comedy
telescopic in this piece.
hebelteleskop is as a weed on ocean's foam
his being of a stream of causes
his thought an instrument
for reproducing telephone messages.
hebelteleskop, teleost. that name included it

Od

teleost perfect bone is hebelteleskop the skeletal of our year as women
ghomeshi case violence against women in his sex his evil

0e

venus, mercury, vanity
being the paradiso of hebelteleskop
hebelteleskop who was didymos judas thomas.
simply a poet of nature, hebelteleskop is making
in the mind of the god substance nature my negro goodnight.
the letter to flora, the medicine chest
divine beings, telescopes, jesus christ,
hebelteleskop, a year in his life
as a woman in the planets
all of this is groovy
vanity of hebelteleskop

Of

the worst long poem, our hebelteleskop.
ghomeshi is a villain and not a good villain as madvillain.
hebelteleskop plays madvillainy making hebelteleskop.
in living the true gods. sleeping in a jar.
the worst long poem, our hebelteleskop.
kurosawa's realism, realism of hebelteleskop. as madlib and doom -
so the collaboration of hebelteleskop and hebelteleskop.

1a

mars
war and peace is a series, hebelteleskop is a series
the tv series war and peace concludes,
hebelteleskop to begin
the long poem as a record album
mixing poetry and prose,
a bad long poem, the great long poem
of the year of the monkey.
hebelteleskop is of montreal, a false priest.
hebelteleskop is in the 514 as mick jenkins (see hebelteleskop 4n)
eating hella poutine.
the long poem is to be made as a record album the phonotext of 2017.
it is a year in his life.

1b

venus
the argument from motion
december 1975
eternally she
ezra pound fucked with kinesis a women's newspaper
what if
UBC ignores rape. UBC vice president eric vogt a rapist sick
sexual hebelteleskop studied anthropology at concordia university he smokes his cannabis became serious as alberta's economic downturn westjet could cut jobs so his slow descent into alcoholism it went something like the new pornographers as a. c. newman he makes the songs they dig the white people and the real canadians
so the hebelteleskop
producing the long poem blending prose and poetry
a record, an epic, the tools of hebelteleskop the microphone, cannabis, the Body and the pen, the telescope, the blizzard is headed for labrador, as the labrador is headed for the matador, that label, his band the labrador releases an album of songs in spanish. so the anthropologist
hebelteleskop mores omnes through his owing their being to cannabis parts of speech coming together this time saw: mushrooms growing on the walls
orange skies
knowing arthur lee
love
hebelteleskop his forever changes
it has turned into crystal
why is this important
killed when their vehicle hit a landmine kills 3 soldiers in mali
his forever changes, the anthropologist
as north korea expands plutonium production they could have enough plutonium

to build nuclear weapons if they push that button as sun ra
so black lives matter
in the eyes of white supremacists
misunderstood hated hebelteleskop
he had his alcohol I have my cannabis this should be crossed out but is
why shouldn't this exist as tender buttons what is the wind what is it
as energy is psychic an infinity of entelechies hebelteleskop sees
from ottawa to vancouver flies and hated who he was until he dies, improving
in purgatory or is this year on planet earth the paradiso of hebeltelekop a
space comedy,
so they found 19 bodies in the dump.
the mind of hebelteleskop,
on tall ships made of snow
as destroyer is integrated into the poem of saskatchewan the negro in
saskatchewan that negro will leave saskatchewan
but carrying in his heart saskatoonies
coins as our love is all of god's money as wilco is integrated into the poem
of the negro in saskatchewan is integrated in [...] are you even a serious
comedian
does anyone in toronto have a pair of waterproof winter boots
this homemade robot hebelteleskop reading tweets #hebelteleskop

1c

those who do not believe in me are exactly like those who do not believe
the earth is round. i exist. an invisible man
hebelteleskop is made invisible. did the zebras make the right call?
the wildebeest
to move through the serengeti
is hebelteleskop black enough
is his life black enough to matter, is hebelteleskop white enough, too white
for you people, you people
is hebelteleskop ethnic fiction?
do you think you're better than hebelteleskop? you're all dirt,
as i have been dirt, as iggy pop has been dirt
hebelteleskop is a better album than the life of pablo
hebelteleskop is a better man than ghomeshi
and yet

1d

as old news, the newspaper
the new york times somebody left on the skytrain, sunday times
so these diamond accents and stainless steel bracelet
as north korea so hebelteleskop
it will launch the long range rocket between sunday and february 14
i kind of wanna be alone on valentine's day and do some molly
or be with u and do some molly
hebelteleskop on drugs
perfume genius the queen of shanghai
as a gay man in america, his personal experiences, so the canadian in pakistan
searching for an underground in karachi
guitar rock sistrum tristram shandy banshee beat leaf house who could win a
rabbit merriweather post pavilion bee thousand here come the warm jets
hebelteleskop knew it all as a negro he strips original works of their
elements, samples the remains he deems useful and engraves them with his
signature
hebelteleskop
we treat each other just like strangers even knowing myself in everyone
as whitman
you hear traces of madlib and j dilla
his humble recollections of the year of the monkey inebriated intricate
structures the biology of the psychology of the hubble telescope as the
serious comedian, he
so the west coast has to do with the east has to destroy the relation parts of
speech in articulation
so that the comedian is recorded before a quiet audience reading his script,
hebelteleskop
inspired by timbaland and mac demarco this celebration of the vanity of the
recording artist, his being in every case hebel meaning vapour or breath
so hebelteleskop is his ecclesiastes his sermon his memories his year of the
monkey his earth wind and fire his animal collective his perfume genius

1e

ethnic fiction
a poem and photographer, a comedian
his space comedy
as they have discovered gravitational waves
in the year of the monkey I am the poem,
this is my Body
these parts of speech in articulation [...] am the fish
charles olson in this bitch
his gravity, his levity in this space comedy
as the work organically
digging the biology of the psychology of the poet
develops, gravitates toward this subject and this and this
as the bee from flower to bright flower too bright
ultralight beam
as he listens
to the light scent
of the buzzing descent precipitation the humanity of his poem
as an alienated
as a black canadian
as a poem of earth, planet of the poet, in space,

1f

as the mind so hebelteleskop wandering now montreal now toronto now vancouver
vancouver the locus of the photographer his focus as hebelteleskop
living using social media writing living as writing
living as writing
believing in the work, knowing
all is vanity as the matter is essentially vapourous,
as neighbouring poets, their influence, as i meditate, observing
the poem never stops
in the year of the monkey
in this goodnight

1g

the poem is aimless and about itself

1h

hebelteleskop is stabbed multiple times, the video is stabbed multiple times,
video is born, video dies tonight he is stabbed multiple times, in
hebeteleskop 0b the video hebelteleskop tonight is stabbed multiple times
survives
that's nature, things in motion, motion in things
the dead bury the dead and it is not very interesting
concise lucid and as well-written as prose
mixing poetry and prose but a stranger will stab hebelteleskop multiple times
ending hebelteleskop in 2022.
yet for now for 2016 there is no end
of things in the heart as pound bursts through.
and the poem is of the photographer and an anthropologist hebelteleskop
studying the long poem
working as an aeration specialist
i played about without
knowing the monkey's sorrowful noise
the butterflies yellow with august as pound's chinese
is this poem effective?
what kind of a poem is this
this isn't shakespeare but thank cannabis for hebelteleskop
he lived his time in canada as an outsider observing history his time living
alone loving the nothingness of the cosmos his vanity vanity of the cosmos
i am the video, the poem, the record album hebelteleskop
living this as writing
as has the readers fallen asleep?
yes, i smoke cannabis
and in 2022 i will be stabbed multiple times by the film critics and literary
critics hated his long poem our hebelteleskop stabbed finally to death passing
out of this paradiso
for the time being (of the monkey)

li

to be assembled in 2017 using his twitter archive
hebelteleskop the long poem, a video documenting the free life of
hebelteleskop his vanity
an anthropology of women, a zumbiology in latin america the metamorphosis of
the crying of lot 49 as hebelteleskop plays books in his shelf into the poem
using incorrectly and correctly the english language following the
hebelteleskop method
life as writing and the epic in its raw
shot and edited together by hebelteleskop
are you even a serious comedian?
hebelteleskop on drugs questioning as I walk through the long poem questioning
as i walk through the long poem questioning
as a serious comedian
the significance of the physical materials his comedic material
as hebelteleskop is the making of hebelteleskop, a video
experiment in the year of hebelteleskop
the fish teleost
this is the twitter archive and experience of the free time of the
anthropologist on the planet surface, his home.

1j

black lives matter
hebelteleskop
underrated in the game
of lo-fi audiobook -making
home video -making, he
should be loved, telescope
far-seeing, the ultimate vanity of all thangs
seeing and using social media of the time
black lives matter
so hebelteleskop is making an epic documentary about how boring his life is
his odyssey
black lives matter
as in the vancouver public library hebelteleskop photographing distant objects
as everything is distant and in space so why not call the video hebelteleskop
his epic
black lives matter
as the poet the anthropology specialist takes from the americans
documenting his free time composing his canadian epic
poetry documentary
black lives matter
the life of @hebelteleskop on twitter
as he takes from the americans
american poetry since 1950 innovators and outsiders, black lives
hebelteleskop an outsider in vancouver
in torontreal
distant, obscure, black, canadian, on the planet surface
photographing distant objects from the planet surface
or as the hubble telescope [...] all of this is groovy
hebelteleskop the movie
a document of his free time in the first world

living as writing
living as thinking as writing

1k

it's racism keeping hebelteleskop down
in a society where all poets are outsiders, hebelteleskop is outside the outside. will it ever be accepted, his documentary hebelteleskop?
an epic of the making of an epic of the making of an epic
hebelteleskop
its being in space, his paradiso, his hebelteleskop
a way of being in the world
a relation to objects as distant
an alienated whitman seeing hebelteleskop in every object
in this video the official text of his long poem
began as a phonotext and became a video as the home videos began to document
the creation of hebelteleskop in the beginning and holy hebel as a video novel
his epic as the naval is contemplated
i was sleeping and saw the context of people
robert creeley
a violin which was following me
jack spicer
the changes that are taking place are so many and so interesting
john cage
as hebelteleskop plays the americans into the epic
his tendency to get hung up on one line another and the other line
of thought from thought to thought as bird from perch to perch to perch
in thought in the hebel dream teleskop as the cops pass the poet, vancouver
being so hip to that torontreal being so hip to that hebelteleskop
in this montage, collage of thought and imagery imaginary of the hebel we see through the telescope
the distance of the objects of the everyday from reality outside of all is vanity,
what is the wind, what is it, what is this.

11

this is the dream speaking
author of my thoughts, god substance
as the comedian of cannabis as the letter c by wallace stevens as he walked
writing as being is always in style a poetics of walking as writing
photography of writing using the light as hebelteleskop walks to hastings and main to buy weed again the professional photographer hebelteleskop supercedes this production and that production
as everything produces in this biological community
as the plants are included in mind informing the composition of this composition of this composition
as the poet's drug use is documented, and the minute figures embedded in history
each one hebelteleskop
all is one hebelteleskop
an epic, ethnic fiction, knowing the physical universe this way, knowing this tao, believing in that which is knowing itself vanity
self-reflexive, -critical
footage bringing you the minimal the bits of information as we are processed by the universe as the universe this is the universe this is time this is the boredom of the poet his hebelteleskop

1m

using digital media to produce an epic documentary
of the drug use of the poet in this,
this is the year of the monkey.
in vancouver this hebelteleskop
on st laurent
he had his alcohol then
i have my cannabis now in this year of the monkey smoking this cannabis on the
way to compose this hebelteleskop
the epic documentary of the boredom of the poet.
this epic documentary of the boredom of the poet
in a moment in which in a moment there will be another moment see another
to see another and another until the last breath
as hebelteleskop is stabbed multiple times by film critics, literary critics
makers relate the bored those who have been there dig it,
the epic documentary of the universal hebelteleskop
his boredom to produce a longer than most documentaries documentary,
uncut poetry, using digital media this way
without direction,

1n

the worst predicted impacts of climate change are starting to happen and much faster than climate scientists expected

10

as hebelteleskop reads from rolling stone magazine
climate change is threatening the arctic monkeys
hebelteleskop an inconvenient documentary epic poem
documenting vancouver the streets [...] the rain
walking to the skytrain station

1p

in this dream familiar and mysterious survey of the surface of mercury
venus its atmosphere speaking using edmund spenser ecclesiastes
delusional his long poem the worst
an epic handmade as the documentary this fictional hebelteleskop
no one is watching
always someone is watching
as the poem is as a weed on ocean's foam
as lord byron is integrated into the video text
his odyssey his space comedy his paradiso
written as didymos judas thomas,
as someone knowing ghomeshi in 2015 disgraced
as the name kurosawa's dropped
as the television series war and peace is dropped into the introductory
minutes of the epic of a year in the life of the fictional hebelteleskop
listening back to the beginning of the poem as he writes hebelteleskop
as he walks to the skytrain station
a mockumentarian
his doc, his epic starring vancouver
the new pornographers love forever changes the black lives matter movement
gertrude stein leibniz dante
these are the cultural references so far in the poem series novel epic poem
this is the experience of the african in his canada as a black canadian an
alien among the hip young people an invisible man is hebelteleskop too white
to be ethnic fiction?
the newspaper a thing of the past
hebelteleskop the north korea of canadian literature
as tristram shandy and animal collective
brian eno guided by voices
he knew it all as a negro in saskatoon
as a poet emulating himself and nature as a photographer of the way
the city ignores the poem as the work organically incorporating his

surroundings develops towards an anthropology of solitude
living as writing in language and light
aimless loveless as my bloody valentine is recalled in this prose poem epic poem recollection aleatory stream of consciousness you could call it his own kind of poem a visual a mobile digital record of his solitude his attitude as hebelteleskop toward his station his being a minute figure embedded in history in cascadia his prayer
praying i'll be somewhere safe when the earthquake we know is happening soon happens when it happens
as seismologists' promises are incorporated into the body of hebelteleskop
as the body of hebelteleskop this the body of hebelteleskop is found,
as the body of hebelteleskop is found
tonight in 2022 the video is stabbed multiple times, the docudramatist

1q

hebelteleskop a docudrama?
is it docudramatic enough to be classed as a docudrama,
black enough to be classed as a black man in canada
is it funny enough his vanity
the docudrama
his drugs and alcohol use his boredom his solitude
as a minute figure embedded in history in vancouver b.c.
watching this special on PBS about the history of the black panther party
feline leisure of panthers
leopards sniffing grape shoots by scupper hole crouched panthers
by forehatch
a delight, the poet, hebelteleskop
his zig zag atmosphere phenoumenal
a wunsch by which
as he tokes
smoking his weed
recording hebelteleskop
photographing distant objects
producing an epic docudrama of the year of the monkey in vancouver b.c. as a
canadian his solitude
using social media to produce
and hebelteleskop
is it docudramatic enough to be classed as a docudrama,
black enough to be classed as a black man in canada
is it funny enough his vanity
the docudrama his drugs and alcohol use his boredom his solitude
as a minute figure embedded in history in vancouver b.c.
no one loves hebelteleskop the docudrama
no one loves hebelteleskop
is it because nothing happens in his life, his epic?
a space comedy hebelteleskop in the year of the monkey

have I already said that
hebelteleskop is a space comedy?
epic docudrama
in this galaxy

1r

performing his free time
as he smokes his
cannabis
this
should be crossed out but is
why shouldn't this exist
hebelteleskop, a space comedy
divine epic, divine am i,
hebelteleskop. today
is a good day to make hebelteleskop
in the year of the monkey

1s

in a society where all poets are outsiders, hebelteleskop is outside the outside. - the long poem as docudrama
to begin

Earth

1t

a space comedy, distant planet earth
the locus vancouver
more exactly
in this galaxy

lu

thank cannabis for hebelteleskop
he lived carelessly his docudrama year,
documenting the performance of his freedom as a telescope, a 0
the docudrama of the freedom, the boredom of hebelteleskop
is to be 12 hours, an epic docudrama
trash his long poem as docudrama, our epic
'elevate' - chatting up
visitors who waited to meet him in an elevator in oxford university
hebelteleskop is better art than 'elevate'
a year in his life, his boredom, his vanity, his epic
more real
guitar superheroes invade vancouver
to save us from the dreaded hebelteleskop
an epic docudrama
as the docudrama and clothing
a progressive dance rock duo wearing hebelteleskop shoes
as hebelteleskop grows
as the docudrama swimming
so hebelteleskop out of the human racism
so the comedy of hebelteleskop
the very funny friend of the anglophone montrealers
the anthropologist, his video

lv

in this docudrama
one dead another injured in avalanche near golden boston pizza's crust
does the docudrama endure as sound and vision?
does anyone read the canadian negro, his tweets, in this docudrama?
to pretend that the person of colour, his epic docudrama, does not exist, so many, i had not thought...

lw

i docudramatize, make the epic, a phonotextual composer, a video docudramatist
who studied cinema video communication at dawson college, anthropology at
concordia university, english literature at the university of british columbia,
his education having a little to do with the way the whole hebelteleskop
experiment goes down smoothly when you guzzle an odwalla
as busdriver lyrics are included in the docudrama, one hour in

1x

and it has been called pure, his paradiso
his team is elated
as the vancouver canucks
hebelteleskop,
docudramatization of the life of the black man in canada
this is the voice-over composed as it is assembled, the docudrama
this is the voice-over composed as tweets as the cannabis user he eternally he takes these tweets arranges this into this hebelteleskop document of the free time of the video in vancouver his cannabis use his drugs and alcoholism his self-reflexivity as a docudramatist things to note
it's me the video, the stoned editor hebelteleskop
better than steven soderbergh - hebelteleskop

ly

as ted berrigan, he flips old materials,
'magnificence of the city sense the buildings and events
et cetera,'
so hebelteleskop:
'as the poets, . anapests and trochees
 and hexameter meter / as perhaps we ought to feel with more imagination in
which the suffering of others and the weather smothers as god watches from the
comfort of his non-existence his bliss which would be ours and minutes away
from death, as the answer to these questions
 lies and discoveries of others before our time together as humans turns as
the poets the truly useless in our culture turns to nature is rescue of the
non-normative modes of speech in balance as creatures precarious
of ridiculous intellect, we applies ourselves and replies in the application
of sophistication is suspicious
 erect to the greek
the voice protects / poem to suspect, to celebrate, as the comic graphic
telltale police compatible coherence of consensus, this poem is the
administration of anesthetic is ours of theirs to lost police time ours is
time as to theirs as the pain is understood truly anyone really knows
breathing ours breathes theirs is burning this
 is a poem about poetry for the poets and the poetry. as the hart crane in
search of lost time again is to be turned loose and in its capture energy
 the poet to be born / we have in common as humans an origin in song and the
pain of absence our symbols
 this is desire as the being everywhere yearns all our lives together sing
human folly and the current events the real truth and impossible also presence
and the voice a consolation
 this poetry is about poetry, the poet is for the poets / this poetry'
this epic documentary hebelteleskop

1z

the god thought the body of man is evolved
to a brain and speech in the dark
as hebelteleskop passes through vancouver streets
forests and over waters speech
and between scylla and charybdis
this should be crossed out but is
why shouldn't this exist
the trails of earth, the pyramid of his life begins to describe what is in him,
beating image off his tongue the blood carrying image through the heart the
blood himself on a lake speech the drum creates itself as the heart sees and
makes itself a life and again a life like the holy sun with us forever then
another past that the god thought arrived sweet seeing and then behind that we
did another thing we began to sing
as amiri baraka is included in the epic
as ted berrigan, he flips old materials
so hebelteleskop the docudrama, improvised
and edited carefully distant planet earth the locus vancouver more exactly, a
space comedy, in this galaxy the poet, the docudramatist
bathes washes himself and in this baptism a new hebelteleskop a new life
every day
as hebelteleskop enters the second month of recording,
hour 2 of hebelteleskop

2a

it is a fucking joke
my hebelteleskop
using the pens and pencils, the papers, the cannabis, the microphone
alcohol, the camera, as hebelteleskop walks through the city
in his free time recording
the longest album ever made of comedy poetry, my friends,
the longest docudrama of its kind, this comedy poetry docudrama,
this epic
this comedy poetry docudrama, this epic,
a long poem, a poem including history, pop culture
glitterbust,
a new collaboration between sonic youth's kim gordon
and alex knost of tomorrow's tulips
glitterbust
have announced their first album, their self-titled debut, a double LP and
cassette release.
glitterbust.

2b

all is vanity,
vanity translating the hebrew hebel
vapour or breath
of the new generation, hebelteleskop, of canada, killing himself
killing himself
people of colour
drinking his wine, composing the tweets
to produce his trash docudrama, his epic poem,
drifting
who to follow
hebelteleskop, let this happen, vancouver, the docudrama, dig it
so hebelteleskop is drunk and playing the docudrama
the classics of the time kanye west death grips
the docudrama can't capture fully really what life was like
african canadian as this fucking sloan plays in the public house
sloan is not as good as hebelteleskop
white people who say i recognize you motherfucker are not as black as hebelteleskop
white people - can you trust them
sloan - can you trust them
canadians is racist, especially the hip canadians
hebelteleskop got properly drunk for the first time in a while and broke his phone so if you want to contact -
what am i doing alive?

2c

eating rose petals ezra pound
no one was paying attention
floating rose petals
no one is watching
who are you
are you nobody too
writing with scissors
writing is
moving pieces of frozen time
good writing
control your ideas
is organic, the vanity of hebelteleskop, what is the purpose of hebelteleskop
you have to go through hebelteleskop to get to the meaning of the text
what is the purpose of this
in your free time you should read shelley's defence of poetry
what i want the poem to be about and what the words i have selected do
control your ideas
a text that is constantly destabilizing itself, the text is constantly
breaking down, being remade, passages lifted from the archives
control your ideas
fascinated by this frozen time
eternally he
hebeteleskop a history
this long irregular poetic sequence the point of it is its irregularity
as pound feels his poem should reflect in its extremely fragmented
construction his being arrested an american taken to u.s. army headquarters

and begins to write the pisan cantos
so hebelteleskop, a man on whom the sun has gone down
his life of small events, pieces of frozen time
a fire engine, a garbage truck, a mcdonald's
the medium is the massage therapy and acupuncture
the content of the poem being the video of frozen hebeteleskop perpetually
moving through the year of the monkey
from starbucks coffee to starbucks coffee
so the human being in its environment, hebelteleskop
in vancouver to compose and again to compose this voice-over, record of the
style of hebelteleskop a way of being in the world, the way eternally he
eternally she eternally they
hebelteleskop is the way
glass of blue fizz
poetry in transit
in this docudrama we call hebelteleskop all the world's a space comedy
we docudramatize using sense organs language technology that's communication,
this is the communication of poetry, a documentary telling it like it is, is
this comedy in space knowing the insignificance of
or the vanity of
as meaningless as fucking stardust hebelteleskop

2d

funerals cremations
next stop templeton drive
vietnamese restaurant
horses records
brazilian bikini wax
osteoporosis diabetes
london drugs pharmacy
sodium chloride
lubricating nasal gel
tiger balm
chinese herbs savoy pub main street liberty market juice bar
the streets ok design east van shoe repair
construction area do not enter

2e

a challenge to the conventions of good photography documenting documentary
making documenting the making of the epic
as hebelteleskop returns home with his alcohol
i have given up cannabis and switched
to alcohol. hebelteleskop is not interested in addictions counselling
hebelteleskop is not interesting
hebelteleskop is quite interesting
a year in the boring life
of a person of colour,

2f

i'm about an hour and twenty minutes into hebelteleskop
no one needs it but it exists
i can do this
i can make the epic as docudrama hebelteleskop
i speak english
i have the technology
hebelteleskop the story of someone of no interest to anyone, someone of colour,
and his documentary, his epic
no one gives a fuck but
at least I've been fucked up at every stage of the making of hebelteleskop
hebelteleskop is a beautiful thing to get hung up on
the meanderings of the poet and cameraman
concrete the roads leading the poet and cameraman the streets
infinity alive in concrete cameraman streets
infinity alive the poet came from infinity.
the poet is the organizing element of the text.
but to have done instead of not doing, this is not vanity
is this - what matters is what you love is what you create
hebelteleskop is a black life and black lives matter
his vanity his hebelteleskop
what do you really need
you don't need his hebelteleskop
but the worst you can do is nothing
his work in vain was not in vain his long poem

2g

composition in photography being the artist's way of directing the audience to
see in a particular way
see as you are directed and listen as poetic composition being the artist's
way of directing the audience to read in a particular way
read these photographic passages and read this
voice-over,
what is he saying?
the most insignificant can provide you with feeling
is this feeling?
hebelteleskop is an outkast
his epic poem his stankonia

2h

Hebelteleskopic Verse

The long poem now, 2016, if it is to stay enjoyable (to me), must emulate the best long poems of our period (John Berryman' s The Dream Songs, Bruce Andrews' Lip Service, Andrew Mbaruk' s Disorganized Thinking and Andrew Mbaruk' s Phono=textual: a novel in mono). This manifesto (section 2h of a long poem in progress, Hebelteleskop) explains how the best long poems of our period are composed. This manifesto, in explaining how the best long poems of our period are composed, enumerates the ways a long poem today should be, the ways hebelteleskopic verse is.

First, the long poem today should be identifiable as a distant relative of the long poem of yesterday (the Odyssey, the Divine Comedy, e.g.), even as it is hebelteleskopic, new, in style. A good example of a long poem identifiable as a distant relative of yesterday' s long poem (even as it is very hebelteleskopic, new, in style) is Lip Service by Bruce Andrews. "Lip Service is my recasting of Dante' s Paradiso," Andrews writes; the poem is divided into ten sections ("Earth," "Moon," "Mercury," "Venus," "Sun," "Mars," "Jupiter," "Saturn," "Fixed Stars" and "Primum Mobile") paralleling Dante' s ascent. The style of the poem could not be more different from Dante' s. The way the poem is made owes more to Ezra Pound' s Cantos. This is a representative passage, from a section of the poem entitled "Venus 10":

> Spoil' s tongue nuns conjoint
>   the bottommost tranquil
>   ebbs furiously jimmied automatons of pleasure
>   are curious trilling sameness - how many men
>   could fuck in the time it took them to think
>   she was gay: our night wide scar
>   anesthesia to the point of morals
>   cherried under law. (128)

Andrews uses in this way throughout the poem anacoluthon, surprising with every line, and within every line, again and again. Andrews in this way follows a hebelteleskopic rule of Charles Olson's: "ONE PERCEPTION MUST IMMEDIATELY AND DIRECTLY LEAD TO A FURTHER PERCEPTION"; "keep it moving as fast as you can" (17). Andrews' anacoluthon keeps it, the poem, moving - from perception to perception, from "the bottommost tranquil / ebbs" immediately to "furiously jimmied automatons of pleasure" and on. The long poem today, the hebelteleskopic long poem (as it follows noticeably the long poem of yesterday) should be made in this way, using if not anacoluthon at least the idea of "one perception" moving "INSTANTER, ON ANOTHER" (Olson 17). Andrew Mbaruk follows the same rule making his long poems. This, e.g., is from a section of his (very hebelteleskopic) sequence Disorganized Thinking:

as in the play
the lines
of the removal
of sequence
in order
directs to the real
brahman/illeity
the intentionality
of the speaker - so
a comedic materialist
e-labour
of EVOL
must cogitate
physically / meditate / mediate
a critical faith
in a beyond ideal ideas as as a poetry / "movement of play
that produces" (Derrida
e-differance is the nonfull, nonsimple o"rigin, it is the structural and
differing origin of [illegible

Mbaruk moves from "the play // the lines" … to equating the Hindu "brahman" and Emmanuel Levinas' "illeity" … to referring either to Amiri Baraka's "In Memory of Radio" or to bpNichol's "Blues" ("e-labour / of EVOL") … to failing to define "e-differance" - every perception immediately and directly leads to a further perception. But what makes Lip Service a greater poem than Disorganized Thinking is its being modelled on part of Dante's long poem, - its being (even as it is very hebelteleskopic, new, in style) identifiably a part of the history of the long poem.

Second, the long poem today can (and should) be confessional. If, as Olson tells us in "Projective Verse," "A poem is energy transferred from where the poet got it (he will have some several causations), by way of the poem itself to, all the way over to, the reader" (16), then (why) shouldn't the reader know, through the poem, those "several causations," the reality of the poet, his or her now? Would that not make the long poem of tomorrow a more interesting, intimate long poem? - to know where the "energy" is coming from?—The great model for the confessional long poem is John Berryman's The Dream Songs, a sequence of 385 "Songs" telling almost a story, the story of a "Henry" who is and isn't the poet (Berryman in a note prefacing the poem declares Henry "not the poet, not me" (ix) but the situations of the character in the poem suggest otherwise). It is only almost a story because the poem is made mostly of lyrical fragments presenting no clear narrative. The Dream Songs, then, is confessional in the same way that Pound's Pisan Cantos is confessional - elements of the poet's life, of the poet's now, appear amidst a controlled chaos, a "chaosmos" (Joyce 118) of fragments. Because the poem is made as a sequence of individual "Songs," Berryman is able continually to digress, - (to write, e.g., a series of "Songs" about the poet Delmore Schwartz,) - to lose the plot - without completely losing the plot.—More similar to Pound's Pisan Cantos (because there is less of a plot, as it remains a confessional poem) is Mbaruk's long poem Phono=textual: a novel in mono. Mbaruk wrote most of Phono=textual : a novel in mono at the Vancouver General Hospital (where he was held against his will, diagnosed with schizophrenia), recorded it (in mono) using a personal computer and office microphone (after he escaped from the hospital) - and published it as a digital album; the text of Phono=textual : a novel in mono incorporates elements of the poet's life, his hospitalization, his schizophrenia, his now - just as Pound's now is incorporated into parts of the Pisan Cantos.—The poet writing a long poem today carrying on the confessional tradition should study these two, then, - The Dream Songs and Phono=textual: a novel in mono.

Third, the long poem today must include the things of today, of the moment, whatever surrounds the poet now - elements from the social network Facebook, e.g., the status updates. Mbaruk's long poem Disorganized Thinking is a sequence of poems written as Facebook status updates. At a point in the long poem, Mbaruk writes "this facebook status is infinitely iterable in the game"

- a status update on the Internet can and should reappear, re-iterated, as poetry - in the game. Mbaruk is assembling a long poem Hebelteleskop, of which this manifesto is part, using his mobile phone, using his tweets, using his Twitter account - using the things of today, of the moment. The long poem today should use new media this way. Just as the typewriter was used by Pound and Olson, in their long poems (the poet would use "the machine as a scoring to his composing, as a script to its vocalization," taking "advantage of the machine's multiple margins, to juxtapose" (Olson 22)) - so the poet today must use today's media, producing new effects, differently controlling his/her words/ideas as the technology allows.—Twitter, e.g., with its limit on the number of characters per tweet, produces a different sort of fragmented composition appropriate to today, appropriate to the long poem Hebelteleskop chronicling (as a montage of tweeted fragments) a year in the life of the poet.—The long poem today can (and should) draw attention to the technologies making it (the typewriter, the mobile phone), as does Disorganized Thinking, allowing typos into the composition, drawing attention to the craziness of the poet, to the use of ten fingers and a keyboard to make the poem. No one else has used the typo in poetry, other than perhaps Charles Bernstein who has experimented with misspelling words, - but the long poem of 2016, post-Disorganized Thinking, must use the typo (if it is in print, and not published as a digital album or as a YouTube video). These are some of the instances of Mbaruk's use of the typo in Disorganized Thinking: "in the galzazxises of infinite racist hate"; "Operate in exoerunebtak farms growing flowers"; "figlfflgiflgfligfigfligflgiflgilfglfigiflgiflgiflgfglgflgifliggl." The typo in these instances shows that the protagonist, the poet, is crazy (Disorganized Thinking is a poem celebrating the schizophrenia of the poet), and creates mystery - what are "exoerunebtak farms"?

Fourth - and finally, most importantly - the long poem today must be crazy and mysterious. The long poem is inevitably crazy if one follows Olson's ideas in "Projective Verse"; to begin with hebel (Hebrew for "the breath") in composition, as Olson prescribes, to begin with "the syllable," "to step back here to this place of the elements and minims of language, is to engage speech where it is […] least logical" (18). Phono=textual: a novel in mono, e.g., as a record of the voice of the poet, is a poem all about the breath, about its own phonotextuality, its being a record of the breathings of the poet - and because its meaning is in the patterning of phonemes more than in the literal senses of the words used, - because it follows Olson' s lead, - it is a crazy poem. "Blue… violet… Brother Antoninus," begins section 1m of Phono=textual: a novel in mono, "Chance… Contortions… In the pants, a Stones Throwaway line… body-subject? Merleau-Ponty… Art, correspondence, production… Correspondence is matter… Dig, there is no mind" (1m) - all of these words are in the poem primarily as pure sound; there is almost no sense but the sound-sense; yes, there are, in this particular passage, references to James Chance and the Contortions, the record label Stones Throw, the horse Throwaway in James Joyce' s novel Ulysses, and to Maurice Merleau-Ponty' s concept of the "body-subject" - but any attempt, for most of the poem, to make cohere fragments such as these leads to madness. The poem is crazy.—Why else must the long poem be crazy? - "to waken ancient longings," Berryman writes in The Dream Songs (in a "Song" beginning "Why then did he make, at such cost, crazy sounds?"), "to remind (of childness), / to make laugh, and to hurt" (200). Berryman' s reasons are good, but does he need reasons? Why shouldn' t the production and the purpose of a long poem be mysterious?—When a poem is mysterious (and crazy) there is no being done with it; we love poems, it can be argued, until we understand them totally.

These four ideas (that the long poem should (even as it is hebelteleskopic, new, in style) be identifiable as a distant relative of the long poem of yesterday, that the long poem should be confessional, that the long poem must include things of the now of the poet, that the long poem must be crazy and mysterious) lead to the making of Hebelteleskop, an epic poem and docudrama. When it is completed in 2017, Hebelteleskop will be made of twelve sections: a proem, ten sections called "Earth," "Moon," "Mercury," "Venus," "Sun," "Mars," "Jupiter," "Saturn," "Fixed Stars" and "Primum Mobile", - and an epilogue; Hebelteleskop follows Lip Service and the Paradiso, is (even as it is hebelteleskopic, new, in style) identifiably a part of the history of the long poem. Hebelteleskop is twelve months in the life of the poet; it is a confessional poem. Hebelteleskop includes things of the now. Hebelteleskop is crazy and mysterious. I call the poetry of Hebelteleskop (a section of which is this manifesto) hebelteleskopic verse. (This is hebelteleskopic verse.) Verse today is at its best when it is hebelteleskopic.

2i

hebelteleskop is as ezra pound @ pisa,
a man on whom the sun has gone down.
hebelteleskop is drinks in the afternoon
hebelteleskop is jokes about suicide, it is his way
hebelteleskop knows what I'm doing and digs it
hebelteleskop is just getting comfortable in its second hour
hebelteleskop would be nothing without youtube
youtube is where in the year of the monkey else would hebelteleskop be found
and loved
no one wants anything to do with a mulatto in this canada
@hebelteleskop is always alone and drinking himself drunk in this canada
in this canada
the freedom of hebelteleskop
i'm not so different from the normal, good people of canada, the whites, those
having a real cool time tonight, the haters of hebelteleskop
i'm not so different from those whose hatred of the mulatto hebelteleskop left
hebelteleskop alone in this great country bummed out
hebelteleskopic verse, it is the way
is the first section earth of hebelteleskop his march madness
it's game day, let's go canucks
so the video beginning at every moment to begin
does hebelteleskop say anything in its beginning ever
a docudramatization of the pointlessness the vanity of his docudrama
the breath his breathings does he use hebeteleskopic verse is his
schizophrenia as he
so the video, it is his 2016 a space comedy
the breath his breathings + far-seeing, that's the seeing meaning from a

hebelteleskopic perspective, as made of the meaningless, as small
everywhere in the middle of a beginning, that's hebelteleskop, ka-boom
as a racist always-already in an eternity he hates hebelteleskop
hating eternally hebelteleskop the critics his schizophrenia his negritude his
tao his hebelteleskopic verse,
hating all of it

Moon

2j

the breath, his breathings
does he use
hebelteleskopic verse
as he
so the video, it is his 2016, a space comedy
hebelteleskop: the breath, his breathings + far-seeing
that's the seeing meaning from a hebelteleskopic perspective, as made of the meaningless, as small
someone of interest to nobody, a person of colour, hebelteleskop
it is a beautiful thing to get hung up on.
so hebelteleskop is on the skytrain underground
digging the being among a crowd,
the video, it goes on, hebelteleskop's alcoholism
hebelteleskop is in paradise
the suicide injury deaths of 3 hockey enforcers
hebelteleskop his online activity
the long term risks of head injuries
these e-mails
head traumas multiple increasing the risk of mental health problems
why don't you dig me
i'm a better man than jian ghomeshi and yet
no one will read this epic docudrama
is it because hebelteleskop is a non-canadian, a black man?
celebrating the small events of his year of the monkey,
this epic docudrama, as a non-canadian, a black man,
as he uses cannabis
just walking around recording vancouver as it was in the year of the monkey
the content of the epic docudrama
does it say nothing?

2k

hebelteleskop ethnic fiction
i'm in the moon, as he walks around vancouver with his camera photographing
the springtime vancouver making his paradiso
the waves i take were sailed before
so it's nothing new, this something new this hebelteleskop
the thirst for the godly realm bore us away
hebelteleskop is not a human being, is an instrument
of god. divine am i, hebelteleskop.
so hebelteleskop is selling a few books, this disorganized thinking...

so those few, the hip, the 1%, whose tastes are towards-the-good,
gather round, read / the long poem at last
as a real tangible disorganized thinking, taste
this poetry, tangent
of the agent of schizolunacy
the moon
so the real glows behind all
is vanity and a chasing after wind. the rich, hip
super-like the homeless. in my philosophy
comedic materialism is this comedy
zumbiologinally aboriginally of the earth-poetry?
so i pray,
feelings as actions -
to be recognized in conversation
in versification as conversation with the other / side
of ours, our conversation, the conversion
of information,
the touch,
the flesh of the earth
in thought, thought in touch
with our phenoumenal world, as spirits
in our being in touch as speech
as our tongue is misused correctly
by the swantologist, in his disorganized thinking, the great work

2m

the most expensive watches are transparent, expose the mechanism of the watch
watch this docudramatic epic poem unfold, exposing the making of hebelteleskop, transparent.
t. s. eliot was depressed at the time of the composition of the waste land, in an unhappy marriage
this is the way it was composed, the making of hebelteleskop
this year of the monkey.
t. s. eliot was influenced by ulysses a modern work structured on ancient narrative
futility, vanity in this contemporary
poetic sequence
the modernist long poem
no unification,
objectivism pure reality, stevens reality is a thing seen by the mind, stevens imagination of fact, the poem of pure reality, cerebral
stevens light, the sun, colour, the poet of perception
incompleteness is one of the characteristics of the modernist long poem
the idea of the sun
notes toward a supreme fiction
division between form and purpose,
precise form, abstract, difficult content
a poem about poetry, a metapoem
a set of organized fragments,
a word is a copy in sound of a nerve stimulus
nietzsche

a belief may be a necessary condition of life and yet be false
stevens
it only matters that i understand the poem
the modernist long poem is about poetry,
the idea of structure, order important to stevens
we make of what we see
the modernist long poem to challenge and disturb,
not a didactic poem
privileges the self, american
olson, selected writings - projective verse
songs of maximus
stevens opposed to w. c. w. and pound
poetry an unofficial view of being, poetry is part of the structure of reality
necessary angel
poet gives to people's lives necessary supreme fictions
stevens content over form
pound form over content
poems we read, lies we need, poems teach us to talk to ourselves
harold bloom
in the canon aspirin section through language the poem all is chosen all together the coexistence of the material the mind no exclusion all opposites
olson a next pound
his didacticism, his certainty confidence
breath shapes how we say the word how we place the word
with the typewriter we can materialize breath
it is all about breathing the poet's spirit, the machine determines the nature of what i write, spirit and machine, the sound is primary meaning secondary
projective verse leads to larger content, larger forms.
ginsberg a beat poet of the beat generation the beats did not try to be literary, academic, an outsider all of them outsiders howl
protesting the times, constructed by breathing as charles olson's poetry
prepare for exam
select passages representative of the particular characteristics of each poet, compare
howl second part an indictment materialism conformity mechanization leading toward war, first part the nightmare, reacting against the culture of the time

moves in and out of a concrete world abstraction like whitman but specifically elevating the outlaw mad americans the irregularity of the poem the irregularity of the people in the poem's world the power of the poem is in the voice the poem becomes liturgical leads to a kind of salvation breaking down conservative bullshit presents salvation through disorder

whitman did this through nature, ginsberg it's disorder, isn't a nature guy

autobiography of red uniting the classical and the modern combines the everyday and the classical as joyce does in ulysses. the remaking of the long poem, accident plays a role in carson's work, the appearance of the text, how the book is designed, affects its meaning.

photography in autobiography of red to freeze in time experience memory made visual

hebelteleskop

exam

comparison

differences and similarities between the texts

theme, structure, heroes, language, style

2n

i didn't really like hebelteleskop when i first heard it
and then one night i pulled it out and all the tumblers clicked into place and my appreciation for it was unlocked
hebelteleskop a docudramatization of the making of a classic record album
tubular bells, thriller, american water, goodnight vienna, hebelteleskop
the adventure of teleost hebelteleskop christ
the making of hebelteleskop as he, t.h.c.,
attends the 2016 abbotsford tulip festival, he tokes
as he teleost our hebelteleskop our christ
as didymos judas thomas he
telling it like it is
all of this is groovy
secret knowledge #hebelteleskop
hebelteleskop is for the city of vancouver, and the world, and for this night
we would like to thank, hebelteleskop and i, the killer whales
killing in this space comedy

2o

hebelteleskop overdosed but did not die thank god
survives to become hegelteleskop.
hegelteleskop brings before man what he himself is
satisfying his need to have what he is in general as the object of his consciousness,
vanity of hegelteleskop,
the project of a minute figure embedded in history, a human knowing appearances, his presence, his epic made possible a kind of collective self-consciousness on the part of the historical community of which it was the expression, thus allowing the transition to be made from the stage of its having an indistinct form of consciousness to the stage
in our people's history in which we begin to gain self-knowledge,
hooked on heroin and painkillers
vanity of hegelteleskop,
the hebel in our hegelteleskop and the hegel in our hebelteleskop

2p

jesus christ, i live in this, a human knowing appearances, moving with spacetime into future flowers, transforming reality with my tools, with the others, composing poetry on a mobile phone - in the imaginary. as we dream - so the real truth of our situation is inaccessible, what of it? - this plant life touches, acts upon me as i behold, is enough already, is a connotation of world peace, if we could just, if only, - so these flowers

2q

ek is besig om te skryf, hebelteleskop
as the frogs, i've got drugs (out of the mist)
so out of the mist, 'n digte mis,
the hebelteleskop translating afrikaans, the christ
maak hom asseblief nie wakker nie.
as justin trudeau, he explains quantum computing, so hebelteleskop
to the reporters
he explains superposition entanglement qubits.
the same love that moves the stars
moves hebelteleskop to read stephen hawking on m-theory,
a family of theories, the current b.s., and decisions of hebelteleskop:
biological processes governed by the same laws
of physics and chemistry, as determined as the orbits of planets.
justin trudeau explains to reporters that there is no mind
the illusion of consciousness
is he not moved by the same love that moves the stars?
hebelteleskop is busy writing
do not wake him (or do)
translating afrikaans always in this passage of spacetime
misunderstanding all he sees
eternally our human being loser exemplar, hebelteleskop

2r

is the voice a hebeteleskopic lens reflecting this history as being one of many?
and the epic
the epic of no one history, every possible version of the universe existing simultaneously / in a quantum superposition? the past and future as a spectrum of possibilities?
the observations you make on a system in the present affect its past.
dig, hebelteleskop is the Body. (see hebelteleskops 3h, 3i, 3k ...)

2s

hebelteleskop is playing bridge whist
boredom of hebelteleskop, in one of the inflatable buildings on the moon,
goodnight everywhere
police say three people are dead
after a collision on dundas street and eaglesfield drive in burlington
dig, there is no death #inthemoon

2t

an iraqi university student in california hebelteleskop
escorted off a southwest airlines flight for having a conversation in arabic
southwest said he was removed for potentially threatening comments made aboard our aircraft and that it does not tolerate discrimination.
we wouldn't remove passengers from flights without a collaborative decision rooted in established procedures
we regret any less than positive experience on board our aircraft

2u

a worldly hebelteleskop
moving in the world from world to world,
 meeting one another and another and
ata befeysbuk? efshar lekabel et mispar haemail shelkha?
learning enough to get by in this world / and the other
ata aliz?
- to include everyone in the epic hebelteleskop
as the poem in the moon, his identity turning in this turning into the verse
into the poem hebelteleskop in hebelteleskop
so that this is his body, this is his blood, his identity fluid,
knowing hebelteleskop in everyone breathing and seeing, becoming

2v

hebelteleskop, a machine of god
as the poet hebelteleskop and the mobile phone hebelteleskop
an instrument of god
an instrument for reproducing telephone messages

2w

oort cloud computing practice and befriended dignifying hybridism rightfully so. youthfully gutenberg droshky cherokee fraternal effort shifty druggist fujitsu sydney dusky diffusivity fuchs. during furry greg shut stringently stretch. stringently stitching study sudbury shrug eternish staggerbush writing stir right seth shrug rush.

eighteenth duty to the runtish furry guy uh. egg sydney shrug fifteenth dutiful strutting branchlet. eternity sheen with shrug cheesy fight you're dutch scurvy wuthering heights and duodenal structuring. eyebright thickest shrug structure fight. structure trudie shrug chairing struggling effect draw rhythmicity rightfully so. whiffling ghetto. exhibiting effervescing dutch surcharging fortify shrug surgery stevedoring hufnagel finfish surfbird guenther. schroeder shrubbery,

vigorish futurity sufficiency shrug rhythmicity. futurology guthrey dusky exterior shrug. dutifully dyed thrush fighting doctor signify. whitney chuckle christy dusky shrink. diffusivity grittier dhoti turbidity sudbury and then we have that shutterbug. shutterbug suffusive turbidities shuttlecocks dogfish disbursing disincentive difficulty's didgeridoo's churchy fiftieth afterthought. futurist fusion they turbidity shirt and thought.

thrush and then shrug first surgery. surfbird churning destruct shrug shrieky staying at the fussing check out of the. stuck check. thrifty they stevedoring why. they they futurity stretch furbish thy. guesswork heywood highbridge devitrify thrifty dysfunction turbidity security tishri thrush distributivity detector first furbish chretien's.

turbidity shut shrug thirteenfold sudbury dreyfus fructify thickest ache.

sufficiency fungi cummerbund fruit salad. churching gushing christening judging. turbidity cushy chef charity,
fungi effective in the rug stuff efficiency shrug scratch surgery third attributes. restrung deducted shrug. detector hell shrieky shred christiansen's turbidity. dogfish hybridism christening futuristic structured druggy dusky succeeding stuffing stationing tinstone scurvy eternish. sudbury redresses gutenberg thundered.
freight thrush distributivity utrecht suckerfish. eyeballing stuck edged furioso duchamp. dustsheet fussbudget fittingness futurology acknowledged that i am churchy shutting vyshinsky.
truer words and turbidities. distributivity detector utrecht university of surfbird sheets figuring digit duffy thrush they'd. subjunctive bushbuck diffusivity and fighting. testifying at fujitsu ductwork church,
thy will be turbidity freeriding duffy fifteenth difficult subjunctive turgidities. pulpy fussbudget duty fight fidgety fishery. righteously check out higher yogurt.
pluto is the shyster duty guest fish. shrieks furniture britisher. mercury in on the shrug. russify they futurity. earth be shrug right hirohito's shatterproof.
deciduous right check curtseying stitched. shrug differently than thrifty scutcheon surjection. shifty futuristics convention. galactic federation fifteenth century shrug gift they fighting in spaces. sight shrug sergeant at the furry had enough
love,
hebelteleskop

2x

killer whales keep doing your thing
not knowing, as the planets... COLD BEER...
hebelteleskop kept doing his thing,
using the mobile phone to compose 2w of our epic docudrama
and speaking it into the office microphone
as hour 3 of the video,
it walks vancouver streets taking pictures back to the editing suite
frozen passages of spacetime, the hebelteleskop
editing together hebelteleskop and hebelteleskop, the minutes of 2x
this homemade robot...

2y

desiring-machines body without organs subject
(intensity=0) (zones of intensity)
schizophrenia paranoia machine célibataire pleasure
assembling hebelteleskop
everything is machines, machines connected to other machines
(the world is will to power and nothing else)
all is vanity hebel desire all is machines
all is vanity and a chasing after wind
the production of reality by machines
and hebelteleskop was one such
and hebelteleskop was his
and hebelteleskop was a real reality really
imaginary, dreaming-machines of the multiverse
in an infinite chain of production
- that's creation

2z

desire in creation / of hebelteleskop, uploading part one of the video
the first two hours and the third hour this hour moving into late april
and producing part two of the video hebelteleskop
live living improvising the docudrama the voice and breathing this way
this way being greater -
we encourage you to submit your own video
the hebelteleskop / managing his energy
his energy -
and in central valley -
the black cat started out as our friendly companion. it charmed our winemaker
until he was convinced its very presence inspired amazing wines
and so the black cat became a symbol
a sign of good luck
filling glasses everywhere with vibrant
as lively as ever
this black cat
this cabernet sauvignon
a pleasant fruity aroma
strong notes of berries, chocolate
and a touch of vanilla

3a

'take care with cannabis
if you choose to use cannabis use it wisely
it only takes a few seconds for your lungs to absorb cannabis
holding in the smoke can cause pain and breathing trouble
holding it in increases the amount of toxic byproducts in your lungs
without greatly increasing the desired effect.
avoid driving for 3 hours after smoking or 6 hours after eating cannabis
mixing with alcohol can cause anxiety, vomiting and fainting'

3b

hebelteleskop uses substances
substances make hebelteleskop
hebelteleskop is the natural, the semiotic
in our being / together as robotic
god hebel dust in spacetime, -
knowing on this 4/20 peace, love and hebelteleskop.
weed, - mushrooms, LSD, - cocaine, - heroin -
hebelteleskop uses all, feels all
deep inside, inside history
(quantum fluctuations led to the creation of tiny universes out of nothing)
in the past always-already
... feeling. spontaneously ...
in every possible way
the universe appeared - hebelteleskop his history,
... identity ...
the substances of the multiverse, the hebelteleskop
my being you being me, same history
same substance(s), hebelteleskop

3c

evelyn tribble and john sutton
cognitive ecology as a framework for shakespearean studies
'cognitive ecology is a fruitful model for shakespearean studies,
early modern literary and cultural history, and theatrical history more widely
cognitive ecologies are the multidimensional contexts in which we remember,
feel, think, sense, communicate, imagine and act often collaboratively on the
fly and in rich ongoing interaction with our environments'
'cognitive ecology
understands cognition not as something happening solely in individual brains
but as the interplay of processes involving minds, bodies, objects and culture
 - no one element central'
'because all elements in this understanding of cognition are interconnected
cognitive ecology focuses on cognitive ecosystems rather than on any one
element'

3d

in this cognitive ecosystem hebelteleskop is the interplay
 of processes involving minds, bodies, objects and culture
the hebel in all
the vanity of 'all is vanity,'
'all is desiring-machines,' 'all is will to power' and (as hebelteleskop,
as the 'all is' of humanity) vanity, this power.
desire, this vanity.
 as the poet,
as desiring-machines, we live bound by these laws.
 & climate change, football, jazz, euphoria
 the myriad facts??
in the dream we docudramatize (interplay of processes)?
('dream' being the illusion of consciousness? are you hip?)
will of that power moving together the world (the god-substance).
(introduce hebelteleskop into your cognitive ecosystem. #hebelteleskop)

3e

in an aeroplane over hebelteleskop
neutral milk motel
vanity of those indie hits, as elephant 6
being thrown into the poem
so hebelteleskop records
the record label of our collective
desiring-production, so dischord records:
nation of ulysses, fugazi,
on hebelteleskop records:
hebelteleskop, hebelteleskop
(all is hebelteleskop in the hebelteleskop reality
this epic record album, essence

3f

hebelteleskop

bibliography

hebelteleskop
edited by david m. schneider and kathleen gough
berkeley university of california press.
hebelteleskop 1969 freud and lacan new left review
hebelteleskop 1970 reading capital london new left books
hebelteleskop, hebelteleskop and hebelteleskop 1970
workers paid off in a thing called love, unpublished manuscript
hebelteleskop, centuries of childhood, london, johnathan cape
hebelteleskop translated by ralph manheim princeton princeton university press.
hebelteleskop 1974 hebelteleskop edited by hebelteleskop and hebelteleskop stanford california stanford university press. hebelteleskop hebelteleskop and hebelteleskop, journal of abnormal and social psychology, hebelteleskop observations on the inhabitants climate soil rivers productions animals and other matters worthy of notice. hebelteleskop the social construction of

reality chicago university of chicago press, hebelteleskop cape town family structure in jamaica harvard university press. hebelteleskop
economic organization ad the positoionf women among the iroquois ehnohistory merican anthpologist coping withoverty in tdominican republc, phd dsertation uniesity of michigan hebelteleskoplife in the trees areader in genal anthropoloy edited byhebelteleskop
stcture sign and lay in th discou of the human scices
1972 jhns hopkins press
socal bhavior of baboons and early man
oxford university press
feminist studies
long term trends of change among the iroquois
the order of things
the negro family in the united states, university of chhicago press
concerning the sexuality of women psychoanlalytic quartlerly sigmund freud female sexuality in the complete works of sigmund freud femininity new introductor lectures in psyoanalysis tposition of women ppearance and reality anthropolical quarterly
toward an nthropology of women
edited by hbeltelskop
woman's role in aboriginal society australian aboriginal studies
political economy of female labour in the capitalist society, unpublished manuscript
woman's role in aborigianl sciency
substance status of women in iroquois policy fore 1784 annual rort of the boar of regents of the mithsonian insuttion r 1932
te denial the vagna
feminine psychology cambridge massuchessets harvard university press
women's liberation as a component part of the proletarian revolution
reinventing anthropology
fundamentals of language roman jakobson
the phallic phase international journal of psychoanalysis aboriginal woman sacred and profane culture theory
primitive woman as nigger or the origin of the human family as viewed through the role of women university of maryland
the insistence of the letter in the unconscious

the signification of the phallus
problems of femininity
rethinking anthropology
coming into being among the australian aborigines,
law and governement of the grand river iroquois
sex gender and society
is femal to male as nature is to culture
stanford caligornia stanford univesity press
engels and women's libreation international socialits review
hebelteleskop housework under capitalism new left review
hebelteleskop 19767 2973 1972 1910 1969 1968
hebelteleskop the omniversous chimpanzee scientific american
thought and language cambridge chssuchessetts m.i.t. press
a black civilization 1937 hebelteleskop
iroquois foods and food preparation memoir of the canada department of mines geological survey
afro-american anthropology hebelteleskop press

3g

drek ahf a shpendel, hebelteleskop,
the anthropologist
assembling the montage, the video of his reading
passages of spacetime
calm, peaceful and focused,
a fucking lunatic -
you didn't want to get in his way
everywhere in the middle
and repeating,
that's the seeing meaning from a cosmic
and as an animal - you know
never again species especial,
in this ecosystem of desiring-machinery,
and as a plant to persist
his purposeful use of cannabis,
as well as alcohol, cocaine and ecstasy
- on this 4/21 of 2016.

3h

we humans we create, we work, we stay busy from birth to death and never rest.
build, aim higher, work harder, accomplish more, and to what end.
this is our time, and holy hebel as the bible hebelteleskop, what do people
gain from all the toil at which they toil under the sun.
all things are wearisome, more than one can express.
it is an unhappy business that god has given to human beings to be busy with.
the hebelteleskop making realities, it has already been;
all was vanity and a feeding on wind,
and there was nothing to be gained under the sun;
the same fate befalls every mind.
the Body
infinity,
as hebelteleskop smokes his cannabis (this too was vanity).

3i

as the multiverse, so hebelteleskop
hebel came from nothing
hebelteleskop is surface artifice,
it is artifice beneath the surface
and on, into infinity, the Body
in our finite, thought, world,
using aripiprazole, clozapine, to produce
 hebelteleskop, a less schizophrenic
more or less good / docudramatization
of a life not as real as the Body
- dig, the *illusion* of consciousness -
and as the man who dies every day
ultravox
so the voice, the process
and the practice of improvisational, long-form poetry
 to bring into the world hebelteleskopic verse
as it evolved
in the year of the monkey,
casually causing hebelteleskops, projects,

3j

and this was one hebelteleskop:
'This sea creature has a remarkable material on it.
appoint women to 50% of his cabinet
"Because it's 2015" pass the heroin. Test this poetry,
quiz this literary material--meet me at the Lobster's.
I do my thing. Like Sinatra. But lesser - and more
than he'd ever been at that time distant
and touching the slain volunteer fighter
I don't pay close attention to the horror. I know the world is horror.
and the super villain to strike again like lightning.
I think that's him coming out now. What are you going to do?
Go back in and shoot him down? Liquid titanium steel. Impossible. Doom, the nations of the world, Purple Rain,
Around the World in a Day, Rock 'n' Roll Nightclub.
You'll bring brighter days. I will rock this microphone.
This is a sea creature with a remarkable material before it, this sapid in this, this real. Stop fucking around.
What the fuck is this bullshit on the radio.
What is it that's happening, representing, it's time, word, it's time,
straight out the fucking dungeons of fiction, this pen lines paper stack, novel of the Poet. it's only right that I was born to use mics. Inhale deep like the words of my breath (Nas).
Taste the novel, best to taste,
test this poetry. No one is writing fiction like this anywhere as the poet a ghost realizing the This creature has This sea creature has -
Smoking blunts with hash'

3k

'Teleost Hebelteleskop Christ makes his Hebelteleskop talk dumb, so that his energy, the physical in our intellectual, is captured, including the assemblage as it is celebrated in the epic, a real care and support for Hebelteleskop.'
so he, t.h.c., made the epic as it is,
the docudrama unbearably long, his epic for the people of earth hebelteleskop.
in 2035 a drought in africa kills 100 million?
as hebelteleskop reads futurevision
in 2016, imagining a hebelteleskop observing his situation, the docudrama.
hebelteleskop got better as the game went on.
it's such hebel the hebelteleskop, his docudrama, his Body
to be in the LUNAR, dig, in our earthly, the PARADISO in our hebel - that was hebelteleskop, temporary in this nothing, that was time.
a long poem mixing prose and poetry
a trash epic celebrating the vanity, the hebel, the physical in our being.

31

black lives matter
and to the white supremacist terrorists
the 3 white poets who turned themselves in, black lives don't matter, white
power - five black lives matter protesters were wounded how will justice be
served? hebelteleskop. three white poets, three white supremacist terrorists
were antagonizing a group of protesters
the men antagonizing the protesters, the white supremacist terrorists
used the 'n-word' ('Nigger')
and one of the men was wearing a mask.
black lives matter. test this poetry
white supremacy of the poetry / of those intellects
as spirit, speaking of the trade, here's hebelteleskop.
write your own phonotext, find materials. white supremacist terrorism:
'three white men firing at black lives matter protesters
against black lives matter are
three white men firing at black lives matter
protesters'
wallace stevens
the police shot 'black lives -' handcuffed, 16 times
white supremacy of the poetry / of those intellects
3 white poets arrested in black lives matter protest shooting the white
supremacist black lives matter never to these white supremacists
but to the poet of hebelteleskop, black lives matter

3m

black lives matter
as in hebelteleskop 1j, as in hebelteleskop 31, in this 3m black lives matter:
hebelteleskop using cannabis in east van,
 a docudranatix, making his words
among the many, as the munuc in our physical therapy together, docudramatizing
his free time in this biome, the paradise of hebelteleskop
what is the use of it?
black lives matter

3n

in our black lives, the matter,
the Body, it has to do with infinity
the nothingness of the [...] hebelteleskop
his picture of reality, the vanity
in his paradiso

Mercury

from the Body, the plants and animals
the realities of every earthly
the illusion (hebelteleskop walking, composing on a mobile phone)
of autonomy, our being in the world (hebelteleskop texting 'from the body')
of the Body, the forms, our knowing ∞ of the Body (texting 'the plants and animals). - is all meaning made
of the meaningless, the hebel, dig, the nothing
of our Body, every possible reality
being *now* as much as any *past* (hebelteleskop questioning every passage of spacetime - is every presence *distance*
is all meaning made - of the meaningless -
by the physicist, - dig, - the unconscious material of spacetime,
of the *language* - ideas (of the Body), the forms,
the humanities, & the realities of every earthly
- in an evolution ('of the LANGUAGE') being / the origin, ∞ , of species?
the ultimate vanity of all thangs? - that hebelteleskopic
in our hebelteleskop!) original bubble bags the Body.
vancouver auto glass the Body, anarchist social space the Body,
occupied coast salish territory the Body, NO PIPELINES the Body,
the Body of hebelteleskop, hebelteleskop and hebelteleskop

3p

hebelteleskop-on-hebelteleskop crime and the death of hebelteleskop.
- the haters of hebelteleskop
they had guns but used machetes
to hack him up
(the LGBT activist,
an english professor, - and
as a danger to himself and others
the schizophrenic
(stabbed multiple times in 2022))
those haters of the Body
those invested in it, the game
(vanity of hebelteleskop, a comedy)
they were to blame.- & as hebelteleskop uses cannabis, - he rolls
one, two, three, four spliffs, - and walks -
so the poet hebelteleskop confused
- hating his poem. - the Body causing the haters of hebelteleskop.
to cause hebelteleskop-on-hebelteleskop crime and the death of hebelteleskop
this too was vanity. - this one goes out to the haters.

3q

hebelteleskop reads into the microphone, into the epic aldous huxley:
however expressive, the symbols can never be the things, the Body.
hebelteleskop: the symbols are of the Body, biological, - dig, the *animal*
in our civilization. - thru the doors of perception,
into the infinity in our biological symbolic and imaginary
in language, - civilized beings wear clothes, - to see
the real / truth of our situation, the Body naked - impossible.
mind at large, the Body, our secret knowledge
and my guide: 'the Dharma-Body is the hedge at the bottom of the garden,' as the spirit
in mercury, hebelteleskop, to learn to be
in Bodily paradise, capturing eternity ...

3r

one bright may morning, hebelteleskop swallowed four-tenths of a gram of mescalin dissolved in half a glass of water …

3s

and if the planet changed and smiled, what then
did hebelteleskop, who by his very nature was given to every sort of change,
become? - as shades, the bright radiance ...
in paradise, in mercury, hebelteleskop
on the planet surface. so the docudrama
in its fourth hour - only under the influence of mescalin
to see what the artist is congenitally equipped to see all the time
(see hebelteleskop 4w)
his perception was not limited to what was biologically or socially useful,
dig, a knowledge of the intrinsic significance of every existent
- the infinity in the hebel in our being and nothingness:

3t

being the Phenoumenon,
the unconscious and the self-conscious
becoming what it is: a nothingness, free in the world,
with a blank canvas on which to create its being
a cosmos
as hebelteleskop reading
into the unconscious Phenoumenon infinity
being for itself, the poem
of hebelteleskop / in the year of the monkey.
this too was vanity.
marijuana, cocaine, mushrooms, LSD, MDMA, heroin,
i use them all, it is vanity.
as high as i am not happy, i walk vancouver streets trippin
in this biome, the paradise of hebelteleskop - what is the use of it?
misunderstanding all he sees, hebelteleskop
 regrets giving $40 to a poet tonight.
an idiot / he could've spent it on Drugs,

'the multiverse - all forms or patterns, it's infinite - dig,
our world form is not a complete expression or manifestation of the divine Reality, - dig, - it is only a fragment of the divine that is manifested in the cosmic process - forms out of infinity, the Body, the idea of the multiverse. dig.
our Body is the idea of the multiverse,
in id, an id idea, the Body, infinity - the divine Reality
a concept (the infinite) physical, the Body infinity. dig,
the vanity, their will to power, the little desiring-machines. dig.'
and they did dig
digging physically-mentally that Ultimate Reality, as 'all these gods are in me' (hebelteleskop) like plato's Eternal Reasons physical for being, dig,
the beyond that is within, our Body, as hebelteleskop practices yoga
at the YMCA, positioning as instructed the body - so hebelteleskop practicing a yoga using cannabis
at home, exploring reality by entering the beyond that is within, our Body, dig,
un earth, a Body
an idea, the id / alive, dig,
dying all the time as time as 'we are time,' - as hebelteleskop
knowing in the present his history (tiny universes out of infinity), his Body (the same infinity, that idea/substance, the hebel within, dig),
making the epic/docudrama celebrating his boring life (black lives matter)
matter being the creature of number, the Body being of infinity,
we docudramatize (hebelteleskop using technology) our position in this,
knowing appearances, imagining meaning living in writing,
using cannabis,

3v

no, not a thing.
hebelteleskop being
a nothingness - dig, his infinite potential! - peeling off the labels,
my negroes...
redistributing these, the sensible we govern,
and in this government,
distortion of the world and the individual
as they 'really' are,
we arrive at a reality,
and in this distortion
is hebelteleskop not a government? every hebelteleskop
a government, a nothingness, a cosmos? - and, dig,
the choreographic in our communal, comrades. and our common values
mindfulness, spirituality, creativity and contribution
- vanity. in this hebelteleskopic utopia,
knowing the act - government, my negroes, - to be like unto
the literary
- and all of it is trash,
even hebelteleskop challenging this 'distribution of the sensible'
in his way knowing the Body everybody's, making our communal
(as these real simulacra, the things themselves,
and hebelteleskop a lone being, move as time (space) unfolds)
hebelteleskop

world’ s largest chimpanzee research facility to release its chimps! in what it is calling the largest resettlement of chimpanzees from a u. s. research center, louisiana’ s new iberia research center announced yesterday that it will move all 220 of its chimps to a sanctuary in blue ridge, georgia! the animals include hebelteleskop and hebelteleskop, freedom of the hebelteleskops! and hebelteleskop, released: 'aum. one should meditate upon this syllable aum, symbol of the Supreme,' and in the face of the chimpanzee to see
our true common Subject, our black Body,
our common I, our universe (and infinity!) - owning this,
everybody's own / everybody zone / the utopia of hebelteleskop -
it's as the Cosmos,' - and hebelteleskop the chimpanzee and epic/docudrama
editing wikipedia: the Universe approximately a second after its formation was a near-ideal black body. the cosmic microwave background radiation observed today is the most perfect black body ever measured in nature
digging the Body, our history/futurity - simply - in our eternally current hebelteleskop, in the now knowing the Brahman in aum …
as hebelteleskop takes hits from the bong …

3x

eternal, the eternalist was to be in a moment eternal always-already,
along his passage of eternal spacetime, the eternalist eternally,
the history-futurity always-already all there? eternally he
dreams in a dream the bad dream of being, the horror.
and he couldn't choose to write otherwise; these are the words It has chosen
- unconscious parts of the brain writing before the conscious?
the freedom of the hebelteleskop, chimpanzee and epic/docudrama,
real illusory shit? the completed poem in 2017 always-already, now.

the Body,
the Raven,
the 'Earth'
in 'World,'
the Trickster
in this Good and Evil,
it has to do with infinity,
our Good and Evil, our consciousness, illusory
the Trickster in our,
- the Earth in our, - Being in the World
as hebelteleskop - 'Gaia!!'
- so the Raven
he Crows
she Crows
to the God who giveth and taketh, the Earth
hebelteleskop celebrates,
the vanity
in our illusions, our live docudramas
as the sensible being governed thus? - all animals enjoy
the illusion of consciousness;
should animals be allowed to govern? - hebelteleskop
governs the animals, eating animals

3z

six million hebelteleskops die in the world every hour in the production of meat, dairy and eggs - as hebelteleskop governs the passages.
teleost hebelteleskop christ conceded that the day may come when hebelteleskops could no longer be justifiably killed for food.
hebelteleskop, his vegan diatribe, his speech, his aum, his docudrama, the peaceful as the niggers, the wholly detached from material consideration, the anthropologist observing
our docudramatic productions of reality, our faithful illusions, eating plants and animals to produce a hebelteleskop 4 U

4a

as hebelteleskop grows, floral and plural, in this biome:
'dig, time and space = cognition and information.
time (cognition) processes space (information), hebelteleskop.'
spacetime = infocognition.
the action and content of the Laws = infocognition, the Body,
our poetry = 'the types and symbols of eternity,'
infocognition = the universe
(a self-configuring, self-processing language)
and christopher langan's cognitive-theoretic model of the universe,
the hebel
(aum)
and hebelteleskop. I the Spirit love you hebelteleskop
you and you you you and you you and you you you you hebelteleskop
communism is togetherness, the mitsein, hebelteleskop.
'veni sancte spiritus'
as hebelteleskop grows, floral and plural, in this biome.

in this biological community: not useless do I deem these quiet sympathies
w/ things that hold an inarticulate language,
emanate the joy of that pure principle of love...
and hebelteleskop: 'It always disappoints me that Aristotle says we can feel friendly toward inanimate objects, but we can't have mutual friendships with them. (E.g., "It would be pretty silly to wish well to wine - at most, we wish that it keeps well, so that we can have it." 1155b30-ish, Nicomachean Ethics).'
and hebelteleskop: 'So we move away from him toward a conception of friendship in which feeling friendly toward inanimate objects already creates a mutual relationship. The objects receive our feelings, our quiet sympathies, and change themselves to us, responding to our reaching out. Not an equal mutuality but mutual nonetheless.'
and maurice merleau-ponty: dig, the friendliness of 'the things themselves,' - their friendly tones and textures:
friendly hardness and friendly softness, friendly roughness and friendly smoothness,
friendly moonlight and friendly sunlight,
these present themselves as 'symbioses,'
as ways the outside has of befriending us and ways we have of meeting this befriendliness - a mutuality, a reciprocity, ...every phenomenon an active, animate entity...

4c

this is hebelteleskop: - aum.
this is hebelteleskop on hylomorphism and evolution: - forms/language
arranging the phonemes, the material of the self-configuring, self-processing
language (the universe) changing ...
and in this transformism,
the evolution - in this
infocognition (see hebelteleskops 4a, 4d, 4e)
alive (unfolding, becoming), a Love -
desires, goals, caring - being, my giraffes
evolving the long neck
to reach the tops of trees, - hebelteleskop.
- that's the Spirit (as we design, form the materials, the phonemes,
the letters (of our creation, our communities) into ...
from one form into another form, every passage of spacetime eternal,
filling the forms, the material - the meaningless -
indeconstructable - the Energy

4d

and hebelteleskop writing her name upon the strand. (HEBELTELESKOP)
hebelteleskop is as a weed on ocean's foam, - his vanity, -
his cognition a part of the greater infocognition/spacetime project
beyond our control; - & digging the eternity / in this passage - dig,
the flowing pointlessness of every spacetime passage, - dig -
and the Nigger - immanent and transcendent, our Body, aum; (HEBELTELESKOP)
that's disorganized thinking - or intelligent design;
infocognition/spacetime, -
the Nigger which resides at the center of every self,
source of hebelteleskop, aum. (HEBELTELESKOP)
who is the real agent in the individual? the all-conditioning yet inscrutable
Nigger is the agent, source of the scientia sacra, aum.
& these are the words She has selected (the Nigger), -
and the atheists: 'white power, bitch,' alas. (HEBELTELESKOP)

4e

'in the field of spirit there is no division; no individuals exist.
so the haters, - if you knew the Body of infocognition (see hebelteleskops 4a, 4c, 4d), you'd love'
as hebelteleskop loved the Nigger, a Nigger lover

4f

and hebelteleskop: 'to read and be conscious of the act of reading is for some men to suffer. I loathe the operation. my eyes are geared for the horizon.'
(the horizon carries the promise of something more, something other -
both the past and the future reside beyond the horizon)
- in the here and now, mindful / of the horizon, of It.

4g

should animals be allowed to govern?
is this butter chicken an injustice?
as hebelteleskop governs the sensible,
owning, eating, enjoying, as an animal.
dig, the criminal / in our biological. (HEBEL)
&: shouldn't trees be able to vote? in this democracy? (TELESKOP)
writing her name upon the strand - vanity -
to be remembered in every passage: It

4h

hebel, breath, the air we forget, the vanity in our hebelteleskop (our community) as we become conscious of the unseen, the meaningless / no longer just a passive backdrop against which human history unfolds but a potentized field of intelligence, our constitution, a set of rules establishing the structure and the fundamental principles of this self-configuring, self-processing language, the Body - its meaninglessness, test
the politics of hebelteleskop, his plant and animal rights activism,
his hebelteleskop. knowing every passage of infocognition always already made up, infocognition/spacetime being
'magic, simultaneous and static,' Energy (delight) in evil (as blake)
cleansing the doors of perception, my gods,
smashing regular consciousness
using plants? (as hebeleteleskop) and hebelteleskop then / he leaves
& brings back comedic materialism? dig. in 1993

COMEDIC MATERIALISM

The Comedic Materialist is writing his Bible--what of it? His way of being, his Tao of Comedic Materialism. It is to be peacefully eternal in this four-dimensional Material Comedic illusion of change, really "in the moment"--knowing the jokes that make up the religion? Really #comedicmaterialism, really now.

~

These are the 10 jokes that make up my religion, Comedic Materialism

1. The God substance, it has to do with infinity. #comedicmaterialism
2. From the God substance, the plants and animals. #comedicmaterialism
3. We receive forms in nature—the idea of a giraffe—numbers, the Infinite. #comedicmaterialism
4. There is no mind - the forms, numbers, the Infinite, the idea of a giraffe, these are produced biologically by the God substance. #comedicmaterialism
5. How did the giraffe' s long neck evolve—in time—to reach the tops of trees? The idea of a giraffe, the giraffe idea evolves. As in a mind. #comedicmaterialism
6. There is an active principle alive in all things. #comedicmaterialism
7. There is no free will, the future already exists. #comedicmaterialism
8. All change and motion is but illusion. #comedicmaterialism
9. Infinite, the space between places, moments. #comedicmaterialism
10. The giraffe is always already in a moment eternal. #comedicmaterialism

~

“This Religion Does Not Match The One Mentioned By Jacob In The Bible.”
Comedic Materialism is Judeo-Christian in its being about the one eternal, the substance God. Frogs, e.g., are constant patterns thereof. Complex undulations of the energy of the universe, the substance God ... an infinity of entelechies. #comedicmaterialism
Patterns out of patterns of infinite nonsense, the one eternal.

#comedicmaterialism
~

Am I the Author of my thoughts? of Comedic Materialism? Of course not. It is the God substance that produces these.
There is no mind. There is only the biological, the neuronal, of the Comedic Material. Of the body.
So the Material is the Author of its own passages, every passage of spacetime eternal. #comedicmaterialism
All change and motion an illusion--real only for the frog, but not to the God in the frog. Dig?
These thoughts are not mine
~

The same Comedic whatever that produces the idea of a rose produces my thoughts
Free your mind, know that there is no mind.
Always already having these thoughts Authored biologically by the Body, these thoughts I think I am myself having
Always already in meditation, observing, as the thoughts happen as they are produced by the Body, as the universe--holographic spacetime-art of the God-substance having to do with a principle outside of all things having to do with infinity alive in all things. #comedicmaterialism
~

The future may as well already exist if our mindless brains are caught up in the web of physical causality so let us mindfully be in the now eternal Knowing the past and future equally to be. Knowing the God substance we are.

~

COMEDIC MATERIALISM

~

Hi

I am very sorry. I will try here to explain myself.

~

Because I am of the universe, I'll begin with the formation of the universe and end in the now, remaining in the now.
1. The God substance, it has to do with infinity.

2. From the God substance, the plants and animals.

3. We receive forms in nature—the idea of a giraffe—numbers, the Infinite. #language

4. There is no mind - the forms, numbers, the Infinite, the idea of a giraffe, these are produced biologically by the God substance.

5. How did the giraffe's long neck evolve—in time—to reach the tops of trees?
The idea of a giraffe, the giraffe idea evolves. As in a mind. #languageofGod

6. There is an active principle alive in all things.

7. There is no free will, the future already exists.

8. All change and motion is but illusion.

9. Infinite, the space between places, moments. So that change and motion are impossible. So that:

10. The giraffe is always already in a moment eternal.

~

I am not the Author of my thoughts. Consider #4,
There is no mind. There is only the biological, the neuronal, of the Material.

I cannot control the processes producing me.
Language, culture - these we do not control, they are produced by the God substance.
It follows that I am a product of the nature/culture of Earth. Of the physical and psychic environment
So, God's facts - these passages out of our control - are to blame for everything.
The #languageofGod of #5 that produces the fact of the giraffe from an idea changing produces these facts, these passages out of our control

All I can do is be in the now, observing my thoughts as they occur, doing always already eternally what I do, changing and accepting this reality as it will have me do -
Knowing all change and motion illusory, knowing every passage of time an eternity.
This is the passage in which a dream prompts me to search for you.
And I find your e-mail address and I compose this e-mail explaining everything.

Jah bless,

Andrew Mbaruk

COMEDIC MATERIALISM

Because the end of 2018 is always already happening in time (God's way of dreaming us, I would note) that while it is around 5 o'clock on December 31st of 1993 in Vancouver eternally, it it is, it is the beginning of time, before there were Materials to be Comedic about. To be Comedic is to be mindful, in the now, meditating, Zen practicing, and knowing the physics of the time--having a Comedic relation to the physical Materials--to use language incorrectly and correctly knowing that there is no mind, only the neuronal--which because physically of the fundamental substance, God,--has to do with infinity. Because our language as biologically logical beings came up out of the God substance and began walking on land and using mathematics came up out of the God substance--and there is no mind. The Globe and Mail is produced biologically. By the God substance, it causes these passages in time and is the first cause and the outside cause--that's Comedic Materialism. Because the beginning of time and the end of 2015 and the end of 2018 exist simultaneously--every passage in it has already been caused By the outside cause which has something to do with infinity and is the fundamental substance making up our reality--that's Comedic Materialism. This is Comedic Materialism--knowing that the time between 11:59 and 12:00 is infinitely divisible, the time between 11:59 and 12:00 infinite, every second infinitely divisible--meaning that it is impossible for time to move from 11:59 to 12:00--so that every moment is eternally itself--infinity in this every passage, every passage of time is itself eternally--that's Comedic Materialism. 1993 is a passage of time eternally itself. 1994 is another passage of time eternally itself--every passage of the two years exists simultaneously and is an eternity. All of spacetime, All Is One moment--the God substance--that's Comedic Materialism. There is no free will, the Comedic Materialist advances. We are to do as we do being ourselves, doing so--in 1981, in 2018, in 2040. Taking the materialism of the time and making it Comedic, making it new and so truly True as to make merry the Material--that's Comedic Materialism. There is nothing that the proper attitude cannot render Comedic--in the sense of there being an intent intuitive toward the Good, as the Comedic is to me Comedy as in the Divine Comedy? are you hip?--so the Materials. Knowing the passages eternal to be "in the language of God" Knowing that God does not care--that's Comedic Materialism. Knowing the God to be the one God substance to do with infinity--that's Comedic Materialism. #comedicmaterialism

COMEDIC MATERIALISM

[H] All entities move and nothing remains still. A frog is ever to be in newer moments,
composing new passages of time itself composed of the God-substance causing these neuronal activities, causing Time. Of the frog, the God substance. #comedicmaterialism
[F] Always already alive and doing, being-in-the-world--the illusion of free will, as we are processed by the universe. In these passages. #comedicmaterialism

[G] Soldiers were on the streets of Paris, and police forces in London, Madrid, Berlin and Istanbul increased their presence as Europeans turned out to celebrate the arrival of 2016. #comedicmaterialism
[A] All change and motion is but illusion—real only for the frog, but not to the God in the frog. Dig? #comedicmaterialism

[B] In one passage the Comedic Materialist practices Comedic Materialism,
in another the user' s overdose, death momentary.
In these passages eternal—all change and motion an illusion. #comedicmaterialism
[E] Always already leaping, making its decisions without Mind—receiving the forms in nature, being in the now—the frog. #comedicmaterialism
[C] Fentanyl was detected in more than a third of British Columbians who died after overdosing on illicit drugs in the past year,
as the deadly opioid believed responsible for at least a dozen deaths in the

past few weeks alone becomes a grimly entrenched scourge in Western Canada. #comedicmaterialism

[D] the Comedic Materialist is to be in the now, knowing its decisions, the Frog knowing all change and motion an illusion—appearing to the Frog this illusion really produced neuronally (All entities move and nothing remains still).#comedicmaterialism

[I] Knowing the forms of speech biological, neuronal—knowing language to be of the God-substance, displacing the either-or structure of the binary—and writing with the body, a user. #comedicmaterialism

[J] There is nothing that the proper attitude cannot render Comedic—Comedic as in all things there is a meaning toward the Good #comedicmaterialism

[L] the Good understood as a biologically produced Good. A "Good" changeable. #comedicmaterialism

[M] Always already playing the game of language, playing with the forms, numbers we receive

[N] from the one God-substance—it has to do with infinity. #comedicmaterialism

[O] always already an animal "in the moment," in the present passage, in a reciprocity with the others, the biome which has to do with infinity--face to face with the infinite, the Other--many others--
being-in-the-world-- #comedicmaterialism

[K] This being the case, how then shall I proceed? #comedicmaterialism

like, it came from outside, beyond - our constitution (see hebelteleskop 4h).
but it's ours! - dig - to interpret. every hebelteleskop being judge and
governor of the sensible, of the structure and fundamental principles of our
reality, the rules - every hebelteleskop the ruler of this, measuring
the flowing pointlessness of every spacetime passage - into points
(a 'point' being the smallest quantity of something, a tiny amount of time),
units of purpose, of meaning - owning, governing, judging the sensible!
and hebelteleskop: 'even the observant animals are aware that we're not very
happily home here in this, our interpreted world' - as the one eternal,
that Body - we are not togetherness, or 'communism,' we are not reinterpreting
the constitution of reality, principles of equality and liberty in
the world, in nature - is forgotten. - what was i saying w/ hebelteleskop?

4k

TRAGIC IDEALISM

1. The God- substance, it needs mind,
To exist, or it is a nothingness.
#tragicidealism

2. Mind is finite, always vanity, always finally wilting #tragicidealism

3. Mind is divided, is a disagreement of pieces in the game
#tragicidealism

4. There is no peace of mind - dig, the struggle, angst of every pigeon , every #tragicidealist

5. Every point (see hebelteleskop 4j) of every passage of spacetime is a memory temporary in this nothing #tragicidealism

6. Comedic materialism is knowing the nirvana in our samsara (or tragic idealism) #tragicidealism

7. The God substance is sublime. #tragicidealism

8. Every angel (or comedic materialist) is terrible, awesome #tragicidealism

9. The #tragicidealist gives fullness to the illusion of free will
#tragicidealism

10. Every mind (or tragic idealist) is a demon, the reflective - and so holy
#tragicidealism

41

#comedicmaterialism and #tragicidealism have hebelteleskop fully confused/enlightened - alive to the nonsense in our sensible, the hebel.
the God substance, it has to do with nirvana #comedicmaterialism
the Body we are, our Body,
the God substance, it is sublime,
infinite nothingness
of Ultimate Reality.
and every comedic materialist
terrible, awesome -
and hebelteleskop a demon,
a tragic idealist? *and* a comedic materialist -
trying to be a comedic materialist, to know the beyond-the-horizon (see hebelteleskop 4f), beyond the words, our tragic ideas - & into the comedic materials - impossible. (#tragicidealism) - always already reading, a judge, a governor #hebelteleskop -

4m

ruling this, ... packaging, selling this (Nigger), these hacked-up / bodies of hebelteleskops, ... Dig, the fucked-up / in our hating the Nigger we are together, the Nigger an infinity out of whom came an energy of forms nonspatial, the infinitesimally small forming the quarks and leptons forming the galaxies, the planets, the clouds, the oceans and mountains - dig,

Dig, the Nigger in our nitrogen oxygen carbon hydrogen compounds forming organisms,
forms in interaction, ideas
Evolving, sequences of the Nigger infinity - every organism, every hebelteleskop a nigger really,
the Nigger behind our animal consciousness (pleasure and pain, our morality and hebelteleskop ruling, judging, packaging and sharing the divided Body

4n

as hebelteleskop listens to mick jenkins,
water more important than the gold.
so it is He who is the water[s]
the O and the H together in this
bullshit. as the H and the He in these
galaxies he sees eternally writing
writing this trash, his hebelteleskop.
in the water, moving
on E, (hit of this roach, get comfortable)
the hebel in this tetrahydrocannabinol,
his pleasure, the justice
his music, the music of mick jenkins
of these spheres these hours of hebelteleskop
the earth, (get high with a nigga one time.)
that feeling something moving, the feeling time,
holding and having, the rings
around hebelteleskop. - around the sun, hebelteleskop.
vortex in time / being / talking all that wordsworth
that auden, that jenkins, the whitman in our Brahman,
all of it. it, being, the soul, of the Body, inside
the poetry the life of this country, its situation in time, that Rome.
the colosseum in our commune, the dream, the biome;
invisible. the hand in this. - playing the hand he was dealt, Hebelteleskop.

40

The tragic ideas do not determine the comedic materials, but the comedic materials determine the tragic ideas.

wordsworth wants to 'teach and delight' the reader.
He wants the reader to learn the poem of Nature.
his meddling intellect misshapes the beauteous forms of things.
wordsworth sees the Source of his poetry as a kind of poem, The Poem.
in Book VI of his Thirteen-Book Prelude, he writes that, crossing the alps, 'with such a book / before our eyes we could not choose but read' (473-474).
In a fragment ('Not useless do I deem'), wordsworth writes about his 'quiet sympathies with things that hold / an inarticulate language' (2-3) - the poem of nature speaks itself to wordsworth; he is referring to the notion of bishop berkeley 'that all natural things are part of a mental 'language' spoken by God' (wu 453).
Nature is 'a book,' a kind of poem, The Poem (see hebeteleskop 1g)
whose true subject - Itself as It is at every given moment - is Being
in the abstract, the vanity of vanities, our Knowing,
& it is co-being and -knowing, it is in our coding. the 'very' substance
being is always. becoming together everywhere hebelteleskop. Knowing

4q

The God/substance is ours. To interpret as Docudramatists, as bEing. History is the liberation of! The hebelteleskops. #comedicmaterialism

4r

vanity of the tragic ideas, our illusory reality.
vanity of the Body, its being an infinite nothingness, the Ultimate Reality.

4s

infinite nothingness, Ultimate Reality, the comedic material,
an energy of forms infinitessimally small, nonspatial. hebelteleskop, you are an infinite nothingess -
the God substance is (without (outside) Mind) an infinite nothingness,
our Body. - our Vanity.
hebelteleskop is to celebrate the Vanity in every production -
Birth of The Cool
Mingus Plays Piano
Hebelteleskop.

4t

Hebelteleskop is at the YMCA, learning about emotions, those feelings Nature gave us (animals) to know the good, what is evil, ?????.
fear, anger, surprise, happiness, sadness, disgust -
emotions causing the Making decisions regarding the ruling of the appearances.
- Knowing and Making, that's Being, hebelteleskop.
All animal-being is emotional, hebelteleskop. Every production
the product of our God-given 'emotionality' (see hebelteleskop 4u)
Learning to be mindful of our emotions at the YMCA, -
all animals moved / by these emotions,
and these emotions (as the animals are) temporary.

4u

Hebelteleskop (producing this trash) Knowing
the impermanence of emotional being-in-the-world,
hebelteleskop being towards death, - as authentic
as a nigger can get, Knowing. ('white power, bitch')
 - every emotion impermanent, - dig, every being
dying - & that is why hebelteleskop is the Way he is!
so hebelteleskop - he must be like hebelteleskop,
learning How to die, mindful of his 'emotionality'
- dig, the directedness / of the emotions
 (moving him to Make Hebeltelekop, his contribution (see hebelteleskop 3v))
- towards the horizon, towards death, towards the earth,
towards the Body,
that infinite nothingness,
- the Comedic in our tragedy, in emotional being-in-the-world.

4v

The emotions, - even sadness and fear,- are comedic;
the tragic ideas are the basis for white supremacy.
don't be a racist follow your heart
It's tragic, the racism in our cooperation using (human) ideas.
It's comedic, the underlying substance
of our equality&liberty, the material.
as hebelteleskop I follow my heart's heart's heart -
I dig the deepest in me, the nonracist, producing hebelteleskop.
hebelteleskop is of the material we all are together, the Body
the Nigger those atheists/racists (hebelteleskops all) love to hate

4w

hebelteleskop is a bad artist, if hebelteleskop is an artist.
his art being
more knowing than poetry. - his brain on cannabis
when he wrote this, - his long poem the comedy
of every earthly anything of hebelteleskop.#hebelteleskop

'Hebelteleskop is Everyman, -woman and -child, simply sharing knowledge together, becoming powerful as it grows (the poem)'
anyone could have written hebelteleskop;
hebelteleskop could have written hebelteleskop - and so he did.

4x

Ferguson, Mo., activist Charles Wade, who has been a prominent figure in the Black Lives Matter movement and is credited with co-founding the nonprofit Operation Help or Hush, was arrested in April and charged with human trafficking and prostitution.

#blacklivesmaterialism celebrates the Body, the infinite nothingness, the hebel in our black lives. human trafficking is not a celebration of the Body, is not#blacklivesmaterialism. It is government of Ghost gone wrong. But as a #blacklivesmaterialist you can make merry the materials.

Every hebelteleskop a Force
for good and evil. #blacklivesmaterialism

4y

to understand hebelteleskop is to Be a force
 against State-force, to Be
the Revolution, (dig, the World Spirit
as Revolution!) the reorganization
 of society, & the dissolution and disappearance of the State. to Be
the Revolution ... or not to Be the Revolution,
to sleep, to be as interpellated, not to be the Body we all Are together
being-in-the-biome, as plants and animals, as black lives, as Matter

to misunderstand hebelteleskop, not to be Making-together as hebelteleskops,
 to own, not to Be / our being together
as bears, as starfish, as Canadians, as moose
 I stick it deep inside because I am loose
as Iggy Pop has remarked.
and hebelteleskop using words to transform the things as they are
into things as they shall be, doing thangs, performing his free time
 as the docudrama, as the flower, unfolds . . . . Dig,

4z

fuck the police. - thank god for every nonviolent moment. - thank god for the water(s). - stay hydrated, fight the power. - communicate. -

every hebelteleskop a governor and communicant, deciding together what is and isn't. changing the climate together - excluding it from bEing?

and policing. regulating, Making regular these materials, the will, - anger, disgust, fear, surprise, happiness and sadness, - in this misrepresentation. - our reading and writing of the Earth.

changing the climate together - excluding it from bEing?

fuck the police. - thank god for every nonviolent moment. - thank god for the water(s). - stay hydrated, fight the power. - communicate. -

5a

a misinterpreted unreality, an infinite nothingness, the Body - that real
being being Being being Being #hebelteleskop
vanity of hebelteleskop, preparing the docudrama for publication -
teaching the docudrama nonviolent communication.
the vanity / every earthly being, the activities - photosynthesis, tennis, &c.

Vanity, the ruling
of the Being, hebelteleskop - the gaze,
dig, the nomination of the visible.
making this valuable, that vanity. Total trash, all of it

5b

diagnosed with schizophrenia and cannabis dependence, hebelteleskop, his paranoid self-consciousness, luv of hebelteleskop for hebelteleskop.
luv of hebelteleskop. dig, the platonic in our chthonic being-dead-together (the same fate befalls every mind). luv of Vancouver, the idea.
luv of stolen land, the materials. - are you hip?
selling His books to buy weed - hebelteleskop.

5c

I'm in It, in this earthly/mercurial Paradiso, -
in the Underworld as buried people, -
and on the Planet Surface as Black Lives, so many

(i had not thought death had undone so many -

fire hits Thailand school dormitory
killing at least 17 girls when they were asleep
in this Commedia, his Hebelteleskop, the horror

I think I am bicycling across an Africa of green and white fields
always, to be near you -

the worst of long poems, his Hebelteleskop.
all things are wearisome, more than one can express.

Hebelteleskop depressed, schizophrenic, dependent on cannabis, suicidal
and killing in this space comedy, -

the same fate befalls every mind (the ideas)
temporary in this nothing, - this nothing, the Body (the material)
infinite

5d

it is victoria day, & it is all time.

& it is as I, Teleost Hebelteleskop Christ, have been saying&writing:

- T.H.C. is Everyman, -woman and -child. #hebelteleskop

- T.H.C. is the earth, - the plants and animals, rocks and minerals, the water[s] - #hebelteleskop

- T.H.C. is a yellow dwarf, - warming the globe, changing the climate, - a red giant, ending the earth, - #hebelteleskop

- T.H.C. is 'the boundless three-dimensional extent in which objects and events have relative position and direction' (Wikipedia). #hebelteleskop

- T.H.C. is ∞ #hebelteleskop

Venus

5e

I (Hebelteleskop) am an invisible man. I am invisible, understand, simply because people refuse to see me.
Ellison describes reconciliation, - solving the problems of Hebelteleskop's existence - ,as 'visibility'
People to see Hebelteleskop, so many. I had not thought …

5f

always dying, hebelteleskop in its fifth hour,
in hebelteleskop, a year in his life.
He wanders from saloon to saloon, - kept on
 living as an alien madman, - writing hebelteleskop.
hebelteleskop in the hospital
writing Phono=textual, causing
the making of Hebelteleskop - about the making of hebelteleskop, his vanity
the fifth hour, his June. -
in a delightful way to be lost
 in space hebelteleskop hurtling, writing this trash epic/docudrama.

5g

carbonated water, sugar/glucose-fructose, caramel colour,
phosphoric acid, natural flavour, caffeine, - these the poet
tastes, - it's hebelteleskop. this is art,
insubstantial this comedic immaterial #vanity,
the fifth hour... of the invisible docudrama.
all the world is a trash epic/docudrama.
his worthlessness. trash of the highest quality.
writing the epic/docudrama without thinking
writing and reading all he writes into an office microphone
the docudrama invisible, no one aboard hebelteleskop
as it touches Venus, - is this no one, hebelteleskop? - the atmosphere
knowing every life vanity and a feeding on wind
knowing this hebelteleskop project vanity and a feeding on wind
knowing that the same fate befalls every mind
knowing the Body a creature of number, knowing every vanity, every life,
a manifestation of the divine Will, of the Body, the Nigger
in this community, knowing every mind nigger in this biological community
this is the product of infinity, this hebelteleskop. this is everything.
creating, as the mind creates the poem, this reality, this hebelteleskop.

5h

no work can stand. - hebelteleskop publishing as Yeats, -
her hand was seized by an unknown power -
what they undertook to do, they brought to pass,
the spirits, - this too was vanity, -
and his system, - a vision, -
the supernatural
in our biological, the gods in me, - 'verily' -
in the 'very' reality
making hebelteleskop - a poem, a docudrama
for the hebelteleskops, - as he uses cannabis
to produce for the hebelteleskops this epic/docudrama
insubstantial, - where is it going? - playing
into the world the record album hebelteleskop, in the cold
of outer space, in the trash sunlight, trash life, and the vanity
of every earthly
(test this poetry) being
the product of infinity, - but no work can stand -
the vanity in hebelteleskop insubstantial, the substance of being
hebelteleskop - in the dark,
(are you hip? - becoming
hebelteleskop? - recurring,
always hebelteleskop, always trash) all seven billion
sparks lost, - (test this vanity) in the endless of time,
as the endless of time, as an infinite nothingness, the God substance we are
really together, you and I, hebelteleskop and hebelteleskop. - #vanity

5i

hebelteleskop is on the Internet - e-hebelteleskop...
'cyphoria' is the belief that the Internet is the real world.
on the Internet, hebelteleskop - a real, artificial, world?
his memory artificial - true, true (hebelteleskop)
to the time in which Hebelteleskop finds her selves immersed,
each a manifestation of the Will, the thing we are. - hebelteleskop...
hebelteleskop is not unique,
individualism out. - in this 'very' 'real' 'world'
the Internet fosters a sense of being one unit among seven billion...
seven billion hebelteleskops in this, every hebelteleskop
a manifestation of the divine Hebelteleskop.
tout le monde le même sentiment ensemble sur l'Internet
'internet addiction is the new intimacy addiction' ? -

5j

the bulk of human activity is the creation and moving of information.
hebelteleskop on the Internet, transporting data.
as hebelteleskop reads the age of earthquakes by shumon basar, douglas coupland and hans ulrich obrist, playing it into the poem,
the digital economy uses 10 per cent of the world's total electricity.
using more and more of the energy, you dig? - the carbon that fuels our electronic life is melting the ice caps. the shifting weight of millions of billions of tons of melting ice is relieving vast gravitational pressure from the earth's crust.
welcome to the age of earthquakes.
we' ve changed the structure of our brains, the structure of our planet - so the book says,
by rewiring our brains on the Internet, we' ve tampered with the old-fashioned organic perception of time
time is moving faster.
as the earth begins to quake,

5k

the Internet makes you reject slower processes invented in times of less technology?
hebelteleskop - a twelve hour docudrama, pages of hebelteleskop slowing it down, to be present
in the age of 'proceleration,' the acceleration of acceleration -
all things in our lives becoming intelligent, things changing too quickly
hebelteleskop in the age of 'proceleration,' making the trash epic/docudrama
as hebelteleskop listens to hip hop, reading the age of earthquakes? - his attention divided
the future is happening, hebelteleskop - the new technologies are on their way, hebelteleskop.
the age of earthquakes is a terrible book, hebelteleskop is a terrible book, the age of earthquakes is hebelteleskop - by hebelteleskop, hebelteleskop and hebelteleskop.

hebelteleskop wrote hebelteleskop to anyone
alone and writing their hebelteleskop,
believing in the work, vanity of vanities, &c.
twelve hours, a year in the life
his year of the monkey, our hebelteleskop. ka-boom.
hebelteleskop was and is. hebelteleskop became
and wasted his life becoming (hebelteleskop).
running out of time, flailing, creating
his epic/docudrama
celebrating the Ultimate Vanity, an infinite nothingness
alive in everything
and using social media to share
his epic/docudrama insubstantial, the poem
makes its meaning in its being
twelve hours of this, this vanity - alive in everything
dead already, - a work of art, a Warhol already,
the meaning in repeating, -
as hebelteleskop explains hebelteleskop
in the poem itself, a metapoem,
the making of the making of an epic/docudrama,
a feeding on wind. Vanity, the meaning in this
power of energy to produce
a day-long video to be installed
in earth. vanity of the poet, vanity of the docudramatist
hebelteleskop. writing essentially nothing in this poem,
essence of being, an infinite nothingness, ka-boom.
power of hebelteleskop

5m

a female artist Hebelteleskop, a person of colour
a female artist, Hebelteleskop, a person of colour
a female artist Hebelteleskop a person of colour
a female artist, Hebelteleskop a person of colour.
a former police official with the san francisco police department.
they are all drug dealers in the tenderloin.
i hate basketball player kobe bryant, fuck that nigger.
an asian, - a vicious racist
they're a pack of wild animals
nothing but racism pure through -
that's a wild animal, I'm going to get him, I'm going to get those N-words
so the police department
something needs to change, bad
code words for gay cops, against black cops,
if we give you that badge, we give you that gun, - that's hebelteleskop
his responsibility -
kobe bryant has expressed in the past that he doesn't much care much for friends and is fairly unconcerned with how he is perceived by the public, and sometimes his teammates. someone who might be a sociopath. loner, selfish, single-minded, arrogant, aloof, relentless, obsessed, ruthless. and your own teammate, steve nash, when asked to describe you in three words: quote, 'motherf***king asshole,'

5n

openly carrying assault rifles, two to protect their family environmentalists. the variety in this I,

50

a user of cannabis
to produce hebelteleskop,
a loner, an epic/docudrama,
 - an alien. in living & listening
up to no good, progressives
talk about the other, as a United tribe?

5p

black lives matter
 intrinsic value.of Hebelteleskop,
celebration
 of the vanity, of It, of I,
the vanity of I and I and I and I and I and I
controlled by currents and chemicals and mysterious oscillations,
 so complex that it will never comprehend itself fully,
Hebelteleskop.

5q

hebelteleskop, a 12-hour docudrama.
 rolling up that smoke.
 I can do this my way,
 the epic/docudrama,
this is the trash of God, the trash sunlight, a black Life

5r

Andrew Mbaruk, an infinite nothingness, ka-boom, power of hebelteleskop.
Andrew Mbaruk is delivered. The animals of his brain.
hebelteleskop, experiment with Andrew Mbaruk
all is Andrew Mbaruk and a feeding on wind.
ashes, dust, trash, hebel
Andrew Mbaruk, Jesus Christ
Remembering the man, his sadness & psychosis, his work.
His generosity, his cannabis use, his comedy.
quiet, gentle, wise, laidback, perceptive, dedicated, consistent & hardworking.
Andrew Mbaruk as boring as his real living as a black man in the Canadas,
#blacklivesmatter

Made in the USA
San Bernardino, CA
28 September 2016